# FAITH

*A Success Guide*

# OVER

*for the Modern Man*

# FEAR

ROBERT LOY

Faith Over Fear
©2021, Robert Loy

ISBN: 978-1-09838-429-6
ISBN eBook: 978-1-09838-430-2

All concepts, thoughts, musings, and opinions in this body of work are the beliefs of my own, and do not represent any specific school of thought. I make no assertions or promises that the recommendations or examples will offer the same success for you as they have given me. I am a student of life, and within this book, I offer examples of ways that life has rewarded me for my thoughts, decisions, and actions. I offer no medical advice and make no guarantees. Please utilize my body of work as another step in your quest for understanding and making the best of this life. Please enjoy, and good luck. Also, anyone is welcome to source my work for their research or writing, but please do not plagiarize my work. Thank you.

First and foremost, thank you to the creator for giving me this life, and always being a source of light and guidance. Thank you to my wife, Kassy for encouraging me and having my best interests at heart. I love you.

Thank you to all my friends, family, and training partners for always encouraging me to be better and for your endless support.

# TABLE OF CONTENTS

# INTRODUCTION: ONE

*"Wisdom adorns riches and softens poverty."*

—SOCRATES

Hello, my name is Rob, and I am a modern man. It has recently come to my attention that men could use a little help, and if this is so, please read on. As a happily married husband of 15 years and father of two young men, entrepreneur, Jiu-Jitsu black belt and professional firefighter & paramedic, I have done many things right. I have worked hard at keeping my mind and body sharp and discovered some valuable information along the way. As a modern world man that understands that the creator has my back, I am manly...or at least that is how I appear to the world in the vibrational vessel I have been given. But the concept of manliness is not just one of outer appearance, no more than a vehicle shell is considered a car or a block building with no walls is considered fire-resistive construction.

There are things going on, on the inside, and that more importantly is what makes the man. Because of what I know and the amazing information I have learned over the years, I feel it is my mission to help those after me to live their best life. Let this book be a guide to your best life, and hopefully one of many. I was inspired to write this book because of all the negative energy being produced during the 2020 months. While many people were afraid and relegated to survival mode because of relentless social engineering, I was empowered, inspired, and grew my business while enhancing my life.

When most people were being torn down and allowing the never-ending barrage of fear to destroy them, we grew and got stronger. I share how I was able to do that within these pages. Writing this book was nothing short of a calling; for the better part of four months, I woke up from my slumber (most likely from theta-wave frequency) with an intense urge to record what was being given to me, possibly from somewhere or something greater than myself, and I felt compelled to write. Also, I am thankful for those that came before me with courage to write about their discoveries too. Without all the generous and loving people that have written books on their great experiences and life's journeys, I would not be in a calm and cheerful place as I am now.

My life has been changed and improved upon because of the words and countless pages I have read on the topic of self-development. One thing I have learned is that there are never enough good books on the subject of my interests. I do not agree with selling affirmations, but I also understand the immense power in them. If you are interested in the life and lessons learned from an everyday man that has discovered the truth to health, wealth, and happiness, then I hope you will enjoy my work, and will perhaps add supplementation to your life.

Lastly, I spent more time "editing and rewriting" this book than I did writing it. I had come to realize, writing and research has become my calling, and I wasn't sure how much information to cram into one book. But after having many chance encounters with other people, and sharing a wealth of opinions and knowledge, I always spoke my personal truth which is I barely know anything (I would often raise my hand and show my thumb and index finger an inch apart for a visual of my meager amount of knowledge). As a first-degree black belt in jiu-jitsu, that has been teaching full time for two and half years, I feel this way too about my knowledge base in that discipline. Despite reading enough books where their titles could fill many index cards, and viewing many hours of film, I still believe I am in the infancy of my learning.

I have always admired thinkers such as Socrates for his humility and willingness to learn more, and that is exactly where my path in life will always take me. I now believe it is our mission as humans, with the gift of consciousness, to encourage one another to maintain a hunger for learning and knowing more. With so many people content in the arrogance of ignorance, believing they know enough, Socrates says, "*Wisdom is knowing how little we know.*" Wisdom is a choice, and I am thankful for the ability to live and learn. Please know we are all in this together, as humans having a human experience, and it's an absolute honor to be sharing my heart and mind with you. Please enjoy, and I sincerely hope you find abundance and love along your journey. Let the journey begin!

*"Men with ideas write books to lift their fellows out of the depths of despair and give them a new start in life."*

—ANDREW CARNEGIE

# INTRODUCTION: PART TWO

*"We need the iron qualities that go with true manhood. We need the positive virtues of resolution, or courage, of indomitable will, of power to do without shrinking the rough work that must always be done."*

—THEODORE ROOSEVELT

To be a man...Well, there are layers upon layers of how to be a man, or at least there should be; so, let us get right into it. Kindness! I believe it truly begins with kindness. But before we get into kindness, we must first approach the topic of manliness. Our modo at our jiu-jitsu studio is "Be kind, Be humble, Be ready!", in order of importance. The concept of toxic masculinity (remember a few years ago they were pushing this agenda on the television) is a complete and utter crock of trash and an odious misconception. The two words, toxic and masculinity do not go together in the same sentence or in a person, yet this is the agenda that was fed to the masses not too long ago. People fear what they do not understand, and true manliness is an enigma, at least in current times it seems to be.

For some reason, long gone are the days of the John Wayne's and Chuck Norris's, though we all still joke about the amazing accomplishments of the latter (there is however footage of Chuck Norris being bested by a jiu-jitsu blackbelt, but more on that later). To some degree this is a good thing, as the portrayal of man as rough and tumble, with not an ounce of internal depth, is not wholly inaccurate. But with the evolution of man and his place in modern society, this is only one layer of what a modern man appears to be. True manliness also represents action, autonomy, and fearlessness, which is what terrifies the establishment and unconfident men. Because when you cannot place a label on something or keep it within the confines of a box, the capacity for growth and power of that thing are endless, and that thing is manliness. The days of wearing flannel, cooking what you kill and chopping up trees to keep your family warm are all but gone, so modern manliness is what we have left. Yes, I know there are still a few out there who can say they still perform these tasks, but only a small percentage, and so much so that they have created "reality" shows to depict such anomalies on television. Interestingly, if you have ever worn flannel while chopping wood, it's as if you have tapped into the inner dimension of man, and the experience feels like home. If you are a city dweller or live nowhere near the woods or a place with trees, I suggest you schedule a vacation somewhere with rural surroundings and try it once or twice in your lifetime.

For what lies ahead, I encourage you to sit back, grab a coffee and let us decode the secrets to manliness together. As for toxic masculinity, yea we will start with that abomination. The word toxic is interesting. By definition, it means: Very harmful or unpleasant or an insidious way. Now let's look up the word masculinity: Qualities or attributes regarded as characteristic of men. So, wouldn't it seem that placing the two definitions side by side would equate to a terrible person, sex aside? Anyone, man, or woman, who is insidious and prone to causing harm, has nothing to do with femininity or masculinity, yet the media and the mind control box on the wall would argue otherwise. If someone displayed a propensity to cause harm or abuse, physical or verbal, to others, then their sex has nothing to do with it; with such behavior, man, or woman, they are a bully and have major character flaws to improve upon. The media and television world (agents of control) are the ones who built this putrid sandwich and served it up hot. Things that make you go hmmm....

Upon searching the internet for the word masculinity, amongst the many disturbing images, was an image of a so-called man wrapped in caution tape with the term "sensitive" adorning him. One can only assume this is also part of the current agenda, to paint the image of a man who wears his feelings literally at the surface of his skin. My wife, who is a beautiful feminine goddess, is more manly than the imposter in said image. As proof, my wife broke her hand practicing Jiu-Jitsu with a student and our wrestling coach, who is much bigger than her. Also, my wife is in her forties, and the coach is in his twenties. I know some men reading this are less manly than this, you cannot fool me, but that is okay. My wife is just that badass. She also lives with a man, gave birth to two young men, and owns two male dogs —that's a lot of men, and all good men.

Are real men sensitive? In certain situations, I would say perhaps, but to make the focus of sensitivity such a poignant aspect of manliness, I believe this to be the mainstream propaganda suggesting this reality. It is not that sensitivity is negative in itself, but too much of anything means the whole is out of balance. When we need rooms to cry in or time outs to pout (remember that word from the 80s —probably not) there may be something wrong with the equilibrium and system at large, and when these are coping mechanisms that grown "men" require to maintain balance, perhaps something is not quite right.

Also, take a second and do an internet search for the word toxic, and most likely you will see a version of a song that, once you are woken up to the brainwashing tactics of the music industry, will further illustrate my point —it's absolute garbage; even the beat on this one is insipid and dull. I can almost see Satan taking tickets at the gate, as the duped masses enter the gates of the underworld, with this mind vomit playing in the background. Don't get me wrong, the tune is certainly a foot tapper, but there is no depth there whatsoever –just symbolism and sugar for the senses.

If you are a man living right now, you are meant to be here. The planet needs good and virtuous men, and with everything going on in the world, the time to stand and be a man has arrived. The year 2020, much like the years leading up to 1776 was the culmination of an energy which led to unfavorable circumstances for most of society. As for the year 2020, the negative energy running things at the highest rung of our three-dimensional world wanted to prove who was in control with a never-ending barrage of fear backed by Orwellian control tactics. For the chosen few, the pipe hitters walking the earth, the contemptuous actions of the aforementioned power players, woke them up, and I think we all know what happens when you wake up the lion. We are going to pull it back a bit though and discuss how we can achieve greatness on this beautiful planet and become better humans in the process, because the creator does not want cruel and dangerous people holding the lines.

Unfortunately, not everyone here, in their mid to later adult years, is here to help raise the vibration of the planet or rise to the occasion. Perhaps that is why so many "mainstream men" in Hollywood have taken to wearing dresses to flaunt their version of masculinity, but to their defense they are actors after all, most with stage names and image altering procedures. I guess I kind of get it, as I agree fabrics used for women's clothing are softer and gentler on the skin. Though this gender bending is nothing new, as young men would play the roles of females during the Elizabethan era; the stage was their version of television in that period of time. My son recently showed me the Instagram of a British (male) singer wearing women's garb with hopes to upset older men, or so that's what the signer said he wished to accomplish. My only response was I enjoy her music. You see, real men do not care if other men want to don women's clothing, while cavorting around and singing about it. That is their right, and if that is how they want to express themselves, I am all for it. But doing so to create a narrative or intentionally insult others may produce a problem. In truth, that image does not present a threat to men at all...literally not one ounce of fear is derived from that. Interestingly, the "men" seen on television screens and celebrity gossip magazines are mere images or in the case of film, "*a series of still photographs on film, projected in rapid succession onto a screen by means of light. Because of the optical phenomenon known as persistence of vision, this gives the illusion of actual, smooth, and continuous movement*." —*definition provided by Britannica.com* So, it would seem giving actual credence to a fictitious representation of men to be somewhat unsound and well, pointless!

Overall, the image is more akin to the Monty Python skit "the lumber-jack song". Also, real men believe in live and let live. If how someone chooses to express themselves does no harm to others, then it does not break natural law, and should be accepted and even encouraged to some degree. That is why I love San Diego so much. Aside from the perfect weather, it is a mixing pot of oddities. Last time we visited, one of the locals was wearing tie-dyed overalls, pirate hat, and had a live parakeet perched on his shoulder —like a hippie pirate. That is fantastic! But many men are here to make a positive impact and have been awakened to the fact that something does not seem right. Furthermore, there are many men that are confused and are not sure what to do. This echoes my thinking in my thirties, prior to discovering that you can literally be and achieve anything you are willing to manifest into your existence...but we will get to that.

Are there men in power who abuse their power and prey on the weak? Absolutely, but I have news for you, these pitiful souls are not manly or masculine. They are manipulators and nothing more, no matter what side of the line they toe. Some so-called men even walk and talk like men, but if they are up to foul and nefarious habits or things behind closed doors like pedophilia and domestic abuse, they are not real men or good people, but toxic indeed. If you judge a man by his bank account and the notches on his belt, then perhaps the definition of manly is nebulous and you need to rethink your motives for reading this book.

This will not be a book about how to bed chicks. There is however a book out there for this purpose, if those are your intentions. I have never read the book, as I heard about it after being married for a number of years, and realizing my game was solid. But again, if your agenda is just to rack up your numbers with the ladies, change your ways or go read something else. I do not want to be part of your seduction inducing sleaze collection. However, no matter how you spin it, true manliness can never be toxic.

So, if the concept of masculinity isn't actually toxic, and can never be, then what is masculinity? I thought you would never ask.

# CHAPTER ONE: KINDNESS

*"If you have the choice between being right
and being kind, choose being kind."*

—DR. WAYNE W. DYER

Let's begin this journey with Kindness. Helping other people whenever you can is manly, and kind. Helping others can take on many forms. If you are walking down the aisles of the store, and you see someone shorter than you trying to grab for something just out of their reach, offer to pluck the item for them. This is a diminutive act of kindness, but the thought of helping another human being is not small. If you are vertically challenged, which does not make anyone unmanly, then you could offer kindness by holding a door for someone or smiling when you speak to a stranger. Utilizing propriety in the form of manners will always exude kindness. The other day, I said hello, with a smile, to anyone that would look at me in the store. You could offer to jump start someone's vehicle or help move a disabled vehicle from the road. You could tip your waitress or waiter well, assuming they treat you well. You could approach your day with the goal to try and make someone else's day better. You could speak softly and kindly to a child. Consoling a friend or family member in time of struggle or loss is very manly. You could offer to wash a friend or family member's vehicle. You could give to a charity or pay for a stranger's meal.

One of my fondest moments of kindness was when I was driving home from teaching jiu-jitsu, and there was a woman at a traffic light holding a sign indicating that she needed money. I drove by her and asked her if she liked the popular chicken restaurant that is not open on Sundays and asked if the deluxe chicken sandwich meal was to her liking. She said yes and appeared excited to be receiving a free meal. I told her I would be back, and then proceeded to purchase a full meal for her. Upon returning with the food, she appeared surprised that I followed through, and she exuded immense gratitude. As I drove away, I felt the surge of giving and love and shed a few tears because I had been on the wavelength of true humanity, and when you are on that frequency there are no words for how good it feels.

Another example, recently (I was driving the ladder truck, for the fire department, which is very manly) we responded to a call for CO in the home. The power had gone out due to trees falling during a violent storm surge. The homeowner had utilized a generator, too close to a window, and CO had leaked into the home. He was using the generator to power the fridge and a fan. It was extremely hot this week, and he had his family and newborn in his home. The homeowner had just purchased the CO detector the week prior. As he was claiming that life had recently turned on him, and he was a victim to bad luck, I reminded him that had he not purchased that CO detector, his entire family probably would never have woken up again; it's all perspective people —but more on that in later chapters.

The next morning, I took a window AC unit to the house. They were not home when I stopped by, so I left it on his porch. He had a ring camera, so I assume he eventually found out I dropped it off. The unit was new, and we had sold two others that we needed, a short while, when our HVAC died. I never saw that unit again and did not expect to.

True giving is expecting nothing in return. Another example, last year on Christmas day, coming off a twenty-four-hour shift, a coworker was told he had to work mandatory overtime because of staffing. With our job, this meant he would not be able to see his family until the next day. My two sons were eleven and thirteen at the time, and no longer believed in Santa, so I offered to work for him for a few hours so he could see his kids that morning. He was thrilled and accepted my time donation. Kindness can oftentimes be as rare as unicorns or common as clouds, it is what we make it as a species. Unfortunately, we have been brainwashed as a species to believe that it's dog eat dog, and every man for himself. But nothing could be further from the truth.

On a more extreme level, during the 2020 virus, citizens were encouraged to call the hotline if they saw people without a mask, or too many vehicles were in the driveway for Thanksgiving. Basically, the public was enticed to tattle on each other. This has happened before, during the Nazi Gestapo informant network, Cuba's committee for the defense of the revolution program, the phoenix program in Vietnam, Obamas "civilian army" and Janet Napolitanos "If you see something, say something" to name a few, but this is appalling. What happened to, we are all in this together? Sure, if you witness a crime or something sinister, take action if you are able, but to tell on your neighbors because they had too many family members in attendance at a holiday gathering, is ludicrous and disturbing. This stunt was recommended by the self-proclaimed elite to create and proliferate fear. Honestly, it's up to us, the general public to keep hope alive, as the elite few running the world benefit more from us when we are divided.

What's incredibly sad yet true is even the animal kingdom understands they are on the same team. We recently purchased a second dog, and our older dog quickly warmed up to the little one and recognized his job was to protect the smaller member of the pack. Somehow dogs understand that they are of the same species and therefore the same team, but as humans, we have been convinced to often compete and turn on each other. Maybe if the media found a way to enter the minds of dogs, this would all change, and they too could be convinced to hate and be divided. Although I have heard sometimes dogs will display racism towards other dogs. However, we do not have the news on in our home, so our pups have not been programmed to hate each other it would seem.

I have utilized the above statement, about being in this together, quite often to describe my opinion on life. As a business owner of a painting/drywall business (formerly) and a Jiu-Jitsu studio, instead of focusing on competing with other businesses, I choose to generate business using the creative mindset, as recommended in the book, The Science of Getting Rich, by Wattles. Instead of buying into the notion of lack, I believe there is enough resources and business for everyone to enjoy success...but more on that later.

As for kindness, not too long ago, I was speaking with the lady in GNC about not wanting to be on her mailing list or part of their payment-based program. I was polite, and told her I respected her sales approach, but her efforts were wasted on me. I do not like to be part of a confusing payment system, and I do not mind vintage business transactions, where I drive to the store, pay for items, and walk out of the store. But I was blatantly kind during our banter. She even said, as if not recognizing real time kindness, no one was kind anymore, as she discussed how she was treated sometimes (This was during mid 2020 during the apocalypse). However, I said, well we are being kind to each other right now, and she agreed.

You see, it is not always just being kind, but you must willingly tune your senses to see and feel it. The earth transmits and proliferates information via vibrations. Everything and everyone is energy and we are frequency creators and receivers, and if you are looking for anything negative, you will find it. This concept is no different than if you are only looking for a certain vehicle when you go driving. If you open your mind and awareness to looking for them, you will notice they are everywhere. This is exactly where the saying, misery loves company, comes from. If you are miserable and believe your life is about being in misery, life will continue to drop the burning bag of crap at your doorstep. We all know the type...the people that hate their job, their spouse, the city they live in and so on. The opposite holds true for kindness and happiness. If you tune into the channel of kindness, you can find it anywhere. Statistically speaking, it is not often someone is rude or discourteous to me, but I do not expect said treatment. I assume most people will treat me like a human being, and I offer the same treatment in return. But I have had many conversations with people like the lady at GNC, where they are tuned into the negative, and sadly most of the population seem to settle on this frequency.

Not long ago, I met a guy in North Carolina, when my family and I were on vacation. During our conversation, he began talking about the few times he had experienced negative interactions with the public. He too was a business owner. Ironically, our conversation was in two parts, as he left to patronize a gas station. Upon his return, he spoke of how the attendant was rude to him. With this interaction, and the more he spoke about his negative experiences, the more I thought he had a propensity for finding the negative. I was in a similar thinking pattern when I was younger but have since come to realize that the statement "it's all in your head" to be completely true. Will some souls find it more difficult than others to figure out the science of kindness...unfortunately, I believe this to be a yes! However, ascending into a kind and gentle human being is never a hopeless endeavor. Is there a time when kindness does not work? Unfortunately, yes. Though I do not believe it a good idea to ever be rude or downright disrespectful, I do however understand the need to sometimes remind people that kindness is not weakness.

For example, we took my son to the emergency room recently because his pinky was dislocated from catching a fast and low thrown football. When the lady at the desk asked which parent wanted to go back with him, I said I would like to since I am a Paramedic and should know how the relocation procedure is done. She unfortunately took this as a pompous response and said in a condescending voice, "Here is your armband Mr. Paramedic." I quickly realized the tension and playfully responded with "Well thank you, desk lady." I was satiated with this, and instantly had closure to our small conversation. In my early adult years, this style of repartee would have led to wasted time and stress. I most likely would not have playfully rebutted, and then been dealing with my own mental resentment. Or sometimes even worse, I would have resorted to my reptilian brain, as many people do, and said something caustic and disrespectful; this too would often lead to me spending hours contemplating if I overreacted. This is the pith and the problem with the reaction then solution modus operandi that most people have been conditioned to perform. Even I am not exempt from this flawed response system, though I am working at it as part of my human journey. Instead, It's much easier to stop the threat, with a playful rebuttal, and maintain your gentle, loving frequency —this took lots of practice to achieve proficiency.

After my son and I went back to his room in the ER, my wife politely told the lady she was a little rude, as I was not trying to imply I knew it all, and perhaps she misunderstood that. She laughed an awkward chuckle before apologizing to my wife. My wife is awesome by the way. These types of interactions happen few and far between, but understanding that kindness is never a weakness, and you still have the right to practice social karate when the moment warrants it, does not mean you are not a good person.

One other situation where I had to verbally defend myself was a while ago, while a coworker from another shift was helping me back the ladder truck, from a scene, after a late and exhausting fire call. As he was spotting me, he started waving his hand for me to turn, and when I did not turn quick enough, he started cussing me out, and I mean he let me have it. The truck was not near anything, to cause any possible damage, when he lost his cool. So, in turn, I allowed some profanity to spill from my mouth instantly without even thinking about it and may have threatened a beating —it's hard to say. The entire situation was a few seconds of madness, but then it was done. My pulse never raced. I never reached the high frequency beta state (which is a very chaotic and stressful place to be) and I held no animosity for the situation or my co-worker. I have read countless books on how to navigate awkward social interactions, and depending on your personality type and conditioning, you can circumnavigate these situations or defensively stop them. Because of all the times others have picked on me, in my younger years, my response system is to stop the threat and stand up to the offense. This is not the right choice for everyone, but I have found it is the best choice for me.

When you have put in over ten thousand hours on the grappling mats, a quick moment of tension does not rock your balance all that much. My captain looked slightly terrified as he walked back to the truck, but no real harm was done from the interaction. It also goes to show, even when you are in shape and the only owner of a jiu-jitsu school in the entire city of 400 employees, that does not mean you are exempt from unfavorable interactions; it's how you internally deal with them that matters. The next day my coworker apologized which augmented my level of respect for him, and we have got along beautifully since. Had I been afraid to stand up for myself, I would have resented this guy and been angry for weeks... maybe longer. Instead, it was over and done within seconds and led to an even stronger friendship.

Kindness does not mean you have to assume weakness or appear meek under duress; so many people have been convinced it does. Sadly, most people forgo their right to engage and stand up for themselves and prefer to talk behind peoples backs or take to the internet to leave negative and sometimes scathing reviews about businesses. Though I do not care if someone speaks ill of me when I am not around, I would much rather them tell me how they feel. But most people choose not to, to avoid conflict. Regarding gossiping about others, it took me many years to learn how to stay out of conversations that involve speaking ill of others, especially in the fire service. It never felt right when I would throw my hat in the ring, so it was a proud moment when I finally generated the courage to just stop doing it. This is still a work in progress, but I get better every day.

I also have not and will never use the internet to hurt a business but am quick to leave great reviews when I am treated well as a customer. If the service is impressive, I will ask for the manager. They always seem a bit on edge until I tell them why I wanted to speak with them. I relish the opportunity to give praise and show my gratitude at restaurants or anywhere there is service involved. If however the service is subpar or the product does not hold up as promised, instead of rushing to the internet with hopes to sink their ratings as a business, I just won't go back... and that is manly. Using the internet to harm a business is cowardly. There are other ways to express your dissatisfaction. If people leaving scathing reviews owned their own businesses, they would understand how damaging this is on a deeper level.

We do live in a passive aggressive society that prefers to shame people and businesses rather than stand up for themselves and quell the problem in real time. Like anything else, it's all about balance. Even Christ had to enter into some light verbal combat here and there to keep people from walking over him. Have you ever been called a hypocrite to your face? It hurts, and Christ said that word to quite a few people. I have to believe there were loads of people leaving interactions with Christ with a quivering lip like *Tim Curry* after receiving a slap from Kevin's mom in Home Alone 2.

Again, kindness and servitude does not mean you have to be meek, mild and timid during social interactions. But the key is to not dwell on the moment either. The quicker you can realize you are dealing with a rascal, and return verbal fire, the quicker you return to being calm and cheerful. For most people holding a convivial nature takes work and practice. Over time, I have learned to stick up for myself, as I would dwell on the situation, and it would eat at me if I felt like I was verbally trampled on during moments like this. With practice, I no longer get excited or upset. After a quip or two, I am quick to smile and return to positive thinking. It's all about boundaries. I also do not like or allow people to use pillow play on me. If someone playfully puts their hands on me, I let them know I do not like it. If it happens again, I let them know there will be consequences, and I would then invite them outside to find out what they are.

I am not a violent person, but I do have an innate desire to defend myself and be the alpha when I am around aggressive or egocentric people. Luckily, when you carry yourself in a calm but confident way, people do not typically want to test the waters. I am still on my journey as a human as well, as I am most likely at the middle of the road for my years on this planet; there is still much for me to learn. My hope is that if enough people would stand up for themselves and quickly traverse situations like these, we could all stop dwelling on the negative and not carry residual stress. When we are all at peace and ease, only then can we exude kindness and love for other beings.

On the flipside, sadly a small percentage of the population will have sociopathic tendencies, and author Ted Dawson estimates that one in every twenty-five members of the population may be a sociopath on some level. Not all are destined to be spreaders of evil and malice like the example mentioned in the film, The Dark Knight by Alfred, where he says, "*some men just want to watch the world burn*". But sadly, some will have this level of malicious intent upon the world. Assuming one in twenty-five people have an underdeveloped conscience, they rely on social clues or modeling to figure out their moral compass. There are certainly levels of empathy as well. I tend to lean deep into the empathetic minefield —when I watched the film *Wonder*, my face hurt from all the crying. If you think crying is for pussies, well it is all in context. If you cry because you stubbed your toe or have a "boo-boo", it may be time to toughen up. But if you cry when you see another human suffer, that is manly, and proof that we are all connected through the divine matrix. Being a father, and human with a heart, that movie Wonder killed me.

Again, assuming that Dawson's estimates are correct, if one in twenty-five people have a lack of feelings or care for others, it's up to the rest of us to keep the bar raised on human interaction to display kindness. One of my great joys of owning and teaching at my martial arts school is that I get to help mold the younger generation. Our slogan, "Be Kind, Be Humble, Be Ready", is repeated and soldered into their little brains after every class. I hate to use the word brainwashing, as that is exactly how society is conditioned to obey and exist in a homogenous system, but that is exactly what it is. Something as powerful as propaganda and brainwashing is often misused for personal gain, but if kindness was the agenda, the world could be a utopia of sorts. On a scientific level, by modeling kindness and love, we are using mirror neurons which are brain cells that are activated when we witness actions and behaviors of others, and this naturally helps to mold those around us. Fatherhood is another chance to implement and proliferate the concept of kindness.

I have two sons, and my (oldest) fourteen-year-old is 165 pounds at 5'11" of a lean young man, and my youngest is hot on his tail. They both have been learning BJJ for over nine years, and my oldest son lifts weights. When he broke/dislocated his pinky finger, he did not even say "ouch"; in fact, he was smiling at how crazy the angle of his finger was. He will soon have the power to create or destroy, and proudly, I have spent countless hours trying to teach him the value of kindness. It trumps everything. That's why it's the first real chapter in this book. My son could completely fail out of school (many great men have), but because he understands kindness, I could work with that and still help him be a successful man. Even if you believe this book to be garbage or rec room fodder, my hope is that you will at least browse this chapter. I don't just talk; I try to emulate good behavior to my sons and youth students.

For one, I, like most life hardened adults, can have a resting angry face, and this can be intimidating for kids. So, I try to always wear a smile while addressing the youth, and make whatever critique I have to make, without adding the extra intimidation. I try to implement positive reinforcement while teaching. I say please and thank you to my wife (or anyone) when she does anything nice or extra for me (which is many times a day), so that my sons see constant kindness in real time. I learned a long time ago that most parents will tell their kids "say thank you" or ask " where are your manners?", because they did not model this behavior enough in front of their kids, so they have to constantly remind them.

Being a child, in the adult driven world, is difficult enough; you really have no rights, even less than the average free citizen, and you are literally smaller than just about everyone else that is not a child. Instead of using fear, intimidation and force to entice and encourage the little ones, use kindness. Because life is one big cycle from beginning to end, and if we want the future adults to understand kindness, we have to model it as adults. Otherwise, kindness will be a lost concept, and we will have no one to blame but ourselves for its extinction. Oh, and might I add, for all the Jesus lovers out there (me included), that the golden rule is love thy neighbor or do unto others as you would have done to you. Also, the Dalai Lama said, *"Our prime purpose in this life is to help others, and if you can't help them, at least don't hurt them."* This is no accident. This is natural law.

If you do no harm to others, most days nothing bad will happen to you. So, imagine taking this a step further and doing great things for others, and helping others…. Now you are not just helping to prevent negative experiences from creeping into your life, but you are helping to curtail bad experiences from affecting other people's lives —like a positive energy doctor, and this is manly. Also, when you help and provide kindness to others, you are tapping into the energy field of the universe. The universe does not care if you believe in the law of vibration or the law of attraction, just like the law of gravity does not care if you do not buy into its ethos. If you jump off a cliff, you will fall until you hit the ground; everyone knows this and will not try to argue its logic. The same logic holds true for the law of vibration and attraction. Unfortunately, this is not taught in schools, but the law is real, and the research is out there to prove it. Look no further than the Sermon on the mount, "*ask and it shall be given, seek and ye shall find, knock and it shall be opened unto you.*" Your thoughts, actions and feelings attract that which is like unto you, so why not start being kind and helping others, so you can attract your best life now.

You want to do something nice and creative for a stranger, and feel amazing in the process? Try the "do a kickflip" challenge. What you do is you go and purchase a brand-new skateboard deck (they are anywhere from 45 to $75 these days, as after tax I just paid 73 for one), and have the shop clerk apply the grip tape. If you order online, this is a free option as well, or you can just apply it yourself. If you live near a skate shop, I suggest you purchase from there, as you are then supporting a local business which is awesome. We do not live near a local skate shop, hence why I purchased it online. Then, next time you see a kid out on a skateboard tell him to do a kickflip. Hopefully, he or she lands the trick, but if they attempt it and don't tell you to bugger off, then give them the board. Then tell them they did a great job and just drive away. My wife and I did this the other day. I had a skateboard deck in my truck, as I grew up skating and would have been blown away in disbelief if someone had done this for me. I was collecting decks in the mid-2000s and had a deck laying around, so that was the one I gave away. I just purchased another one a few minutes ago, online, so that we can do it again. There are other awesome things you can do for strangers, that were mentioned in the chapter, but this is a fun one. Though, I may have to up the ante and purchase a bike to create a "do a bunny hop" challenge, as I have not seen many skaters out lately, but many on bikes. Either way, I promise you this is a fun one. Enjoy and share kindness.

# CHAPTER TWO: LAW OF ATTRACTION

*"If you want to find the Secret to the universe, you need to think in terms of energy, frequency and vibration."*

—NIKOLA TESLA

Most of us have heard the statement, what goes around comes around, or talk about good or bad karma. In essence, when we speak like this, we are talking about the law of attraction, but only at a base level. Even fewer people may have heard that which you think about you bring about, or like attracts like. These are not just man-made principals; this is a direct correlation to the law of vibration. We are all energy.

Albert Einstein said, *"Everything is energy and that's all there is to it. Match the frequency of the reality you want and you cannot help but get that reality. It cannot be any other way. This is no philosophy. This is physics."*

Einstein questioned everything and went on to become the father of modern physics. He was not special, as modern consensus would have you believe. It is easier and more fitting for mainstream society to have you believe Einstein was an outlier, and his intangible intelligence was why he achieved more than you or I are capable of, than allow the truth —he was a man of average intelligence that had a dogged desire to understand life and existence on a deeper level, and he never quit learning and therefore growing. Also, his greatness is not beyond what you or I could accomplish. He was willing to look left when everyone else was told to look right, and early on in his life he realized the stifling and homogenous nature of school and society and crawled out of the box. Also, he understood the law of attraction and energy. This is the basis of what quantum physics is all about.

When you look at anything under a microscope, there are particles that are constantly in motion. It doesn't matter if the object you are magnifying is a cinder block, or your leg. It is all energy in motion at different speeds and intensities. Also, there have been countless studies that prove electrons react differently when being observed in the quantum field, and that the old model of the atom is outdated. Because the atom is 99.9999999 percent empty space (which leads to unlimited potential within said space), and electrons react when they are observed, this realization supports the concept that what you think or believe is what you see. *Joe Dispenza*, in the book *Becoming Supernatural*, states this about the electron, that basically it remains potential energy until it is observed. Dispenza explains in vivid detail the science behind quantum physics and the law of attraction, and how the immense capabilities of human potential are derived from this discovery. I highly recommend reading his work for a deeper view and understanding.

I have studied (on my own) some amazing people *Jake Ducey, Bob Proctor, Napoleon Hill, Rhonda Byrne, Wallace Wattles, Gregg Braden, Joe Dispenza, James Allen and Earl Nightingale* to name a few. Every one of these successful authors/thinkers agree that what we think about we bring about; therefore, they believe and understand the law of attraction. Jesus tried to exemplify this fact to an extreme degree, but most of us cannot contain and control our own thoughts well enough to focus on what we want or want to change in our own lives.

On the low end, the average person has over 6000 thoughts a day, and most are leftover thoughts from days prior. With all the distractions in our lives, it is nearly impossible to focus all those thoughts into one single objective. Jesus could, and therefore could create "miracles".

Jesus was trying to teach us this because he loved mankind and wanted man to live his best life. Jesus was so good at controlling and manipulating energy and frequency, his feats were considered miracles by those who observed them. The famous Tibetan Yogi Milarepa also demonstrated this ability to create miracles when he used his hand to manipulate energy or ostensibly matter and create an indelible handprint in the cave all those years ago. These were considered miracles because most of us cannot get out of our way long enough to materialize what we want in life, and therefore typically receive and achieve on autopilot. So thankfully, there have been others to inspire and remind us of our true power along the way.

I was first introduced to the law of attraction around 2017, when I watched the movie *The Secret*. After letting that movie sink in, and thinking about it, I began to envision health and wealth, and quick and immense changes took place in my life. Around this time, I was making slightly less than 50,000 a year as a firefighter and working my painting business (which I no longer enjoyed) on my off days. I also racked up hefty credit card debt during the transition to my next business venture because we had also just built an addition on our home and replaced our $40,000 bulk head a few years prior. Because of my natural desire to be different, and discovering the secret, I started to see how many people had chosen to remain still and believe that they were stuck.

One of my friends had been in the fire service and worked for a small department. He had never played the parlor games that went on in this department, so the apogee of his career was him being three years from retirement with no promotion or high deeds to show for it. He would spend about twenty minutes in the morning checking off his truck and work equipment and then be on the couch playing on his phone until bedtime. To the untrained observer, this guy appeared lazy and unmotivated. But upon further scrutiny, I realized he had been a part of this small-town department political system, and over time, the motivation and ambition had been beaten out of him, one roadblock at a time. I knew countless others who felt stuck and were just waiting to age long enough to make their exit from the current existence they loathed. I saw this as writing on the wall and decided this would not be my future.

Back to my awakening, within just over a year and half, and during the pandemonium of 2020, we transitioned to owning a jiu-jitsu studio with over 120 paying students and making 10,000 more as a firefighter because of having the courage to leave the small department. Our credit card was paid off at this time as well. Also, I was one of the main ladder drivers at my station, a senior firefighter and paramedic/FTO. I was still able to paint here and there if I wanted to make a few extra bucks, but I did not have to. During the editing/rewriting phase of this book, (February - April 2021) my wife just received word that she has secured a government job that will allow her to telework, earning more money than I do at the fire department. For about six months leading up to this moment, both her and I had a figure of a yearly gross income in our heads, and with my fire salary, her job and the profits from the studio, we are now making this much annually. This is no accident. This is the law of attraction at work.

Our thoughts create a frequency, a vibration. Our hearts also create a frequency; it's why you can read anyone's heart rhythm on an EKG and see the frequency and brain activity during a brain scan. When you first think about something, it is only a thought. But as the thoughts gain momentum and feelings, they begin to gain energy. If you think about it, begin to believe (by attaching feeling to it) in it and then act on it, you are then completing the cycle of the law of vibration. This is the "secret" that the film the *Secret* was about. Where the movie the *Secret* got it wrong, or at least what was not quite explained (they have since realized and tried to rectify this) is that you cannot just sit around and think about what you want and expect it to materialize. Lots of skeptics and naysayers took this as gospel and wrote the message off completely. But the law of attraction is the law of vibration, and it must be followed up with tangible action. No matter how bad you want something, just thinking about it will never be enough. If you can clear your mind, control your thoughts, and get out of your own way, circumstances and events will unfold for you in a way that makes your vision a possibility, but you will always need to follow with action. I could have dreamed all I wanted about owning another business and relished the joys and highs of meeting so many new people and teaching Jiu-Jitsu. But if I never would have taken action to find the space, create a logo, write a curriculum, find the mats and furnishings, and open the doors, then it would have died with me, as a dream.

I spent many nights at home meditating and envisioning full mats at the studio, and now the weekly sentiment from our students is, "When are we taking the wall out, and expanding?" —because those thoughts have become reality.

I have had the pleasure of knowing many others who personally have accomplished their goals and dreams because of their knowledge of this wonderful facet of our reality. I was just speaking to a friend today who is now the chief for the fire department he works for, and he was praising the law of attraction for changing his life in tremendous ways. Also, he appears to be genuinely happy. God wants us all to live amazing and abundant lives, and he allows us free will to choose exactly how we want our lives to be. With the fork in the road between faith and fear, we are all allowed the freedom to choose.

Many of my friends have told me they would like to do this or that, but they lack time or motivation. I have friends who are on the verge of total mental collapse due to their choices and unwillingness to change or take a risk. What this means is, In the distant future, when they are running low for years, they will look back and possibly have regrets —they will have no one to blame but themselves. The thought of this frightens me more than the thought of failure. What a waste to be near your deathbed and leave this amazing world with regrets. You see this is also why the message in the secret was succinct, and genius. The study of the law of attraction is deep and too heavy for many people, at least at first. If *The Secret* had hit the general public with too much information, it may have scared more people away, and may have seemed like science fiction to the incredulous observer.

The journey of enlightenment has to start somewhere, and the cosmos know it isn't prudent or feasible to go from zero to *Mark Passio or David Icke*; although both freethinkers reside pretty deep in the rabbit hole of enlighten-ment. Reading these two, you quickly realize a "conspiracy theorist" is will-ing to imbibe other information than what the handful of news providers are feeding us. I am over three years into my study, and I am learning about different scientific experiments that prove atoms can change action based on who is watching them, even when separated in distance by hundreds of miles.

There is proof that atoms, molecules, cells and tissues all have an energy field, and there are countless stories of how people who have received organ transplants often take on characteristics or preferences from the previous organ donor's personality or energy. In the book, *A Change of Heart*, by Claire Sylvia, after receiving a heart transplant, she explains how she began to enjoy foods that she did not enjoy prior to receiving her donors' heart, but that the family of the donor confirmed he had loved those foods. This is incredible.

It is also no coincidence that people with amputated limbs have reported that they have sensations and feel the limb as if it still exists; they have dubbed this "phantom limb" sensation. This is the brain and body communicating via chemicals, sensations, and vibrations. The universe and God want you to be successful, and you can have anything you want. But therein lies the dilemma…. For if you think negative thoughts, and take negative actions, then you can bring negative experiences into your life. Also, when you set your sights on something you want, you must keep thinking about that thing, not the opposite of or a lack of it.

*Charles F. Haanel* writes, "*You cannot entertain weak, harmful, negative thoughts ten hours a day and expect to bring about beautiful, strong and harmonious conditions by ten minutes of strong, positive, creative thought.*" This exemplifies why most people will quit on themselves and fail to realize their full manifesting potential, as they do not take control, like most of society with their thinking. Think about how many people fail at dieting. Mental dieting is no different. Instead of dieting, you have to change the way you eat for lasting results, just like the way you think. Also, your desires should never cause harm or manipulate other people. If you understand natural law, you will learn that this is universal law. If you intentionally cause harm or attempt to tarnish someone else's reputation for example, this will eventually happen to you. This would be the widely recognized axiom, what goes around comes around! Also, according to Steel Magnate and Billionaire *Andrew Carnegie*, in speaking to *Napoleon Hill* in the book How to Own Your Own Mind, he says basically that human relationships and harmony with others creates growth, wealth and riches. Throughout your life journey, you will need the counsel of other people. So, keep your intentions free of malice or ill intention, and know that you cannot force anyone else to adapt to your desires. It is just as easy to lose momentum as it is to gain it. Once you have something in your mind that you want, you must keep the thoughts of owning it in the forefront of your brain. We have free will, and we are free to choose whatever experiences we want.

You see, we are not given credit as creators, and most people will conform to what society deems the norm —you know, go to school, get a job, get married, pay your bills, raise your kids, and repeat, and no matter what, do not rock the boat. Most people will do just the aforementioned and nothing more, which is fine, but if this is you, you are part of the system... another cog in the wheel. Ultimately though, we are capable of so much more. Advancements would not occur otherwise. Look around next time you are out driving or walking around. There are ideas and creation in solid form everywhere. Every one of the businesses or inventions you see and enjoy daily, were once a thought in someone's head.

According to *Napoleon Hill* and the *Devil in Outwitting the Devil,* only two percent of the population is not driven or hindered by fear. Therefore, 98 percent of the public will find reasons to cancel or quit on their dreams and find a secure and comfortable job out of fear of failure or the unknown. The businesses you patronize and the provisions you use on the daily, were created by the two percent of the population that followed through on their ideas. This is also why many feel you must guard your dreams and wishes, as others will typically write it off as fanciful or wishful thinking... or worse, they may plagiarize your ideas entirely. Unfortunately, this is a true statement, and *Ben Franklin* warns us of this with his statement, "*If you would keep your secret from an enemy, tell it not to a friend."*

We have become a herd society, and it is extremely difficult to stand alone, hence why so few will ever really join the two percenters. But if you are one of the few who can ask without desperation or hope and be "surrounded" by your desires and be "enveloped" by the result, your power to manifest will be something you can control with ease.

*Napoleon Hill* is considered the godfather of self-help and development, as he lived with and studied the wealthiest people of his time for over twenty years, and they all agreed on the importance of our thoughts married with action to achieve great things and acquire riches—basically they agreed on the "secret". They also agreed on the notion of giving back. The universe speaks in the language of emotion, and it feels good to give. Love and care for others is what links us together as a species; the universe understands the vibration of love. I believe therefore there are so many books on the topic, because it actually works, and we are all excited to share its (our inherent) power. I absolutely agree, as books have allowed me to open my eyes and see the world in a whole new light and make great strides in my life.

I urge you to try an experiment. I was recently reading the book *E-Squared by Pam Grout*, which is a wonderful book. In her book, she does a wonderful job explaining the law of attraction, and she offers a great experiment, that she playfully dubbed "The Dude Abides Principle", to prove the universe and God are with you and have your best interests in mind. Give your guardian angel, or your inner being rather, forty-eight hours to make its presence known. In that time, surrender your opinions or beliefs and be open minded and ready to receive whatever sign comes your way. She gives examples in the book of different ways people were affected, but every person she mentions received a sign. I too tried this experiment. At this point, it was December of 2020, and in Virginia we had just been told, again, by our Governor that we are to act like adults but be treated like children for the sake of humankind. To say, tensions were a little thick in the world would be putting it lightly. However, I was feeling uncertain. So, I asked for a sign.

I wrote in my book for the universe and God to please show me a sign to help me know if I was moving in the right direction or just to show me that they were here. This was a Wednesday at 7:55 pm; I was at the fire station when I wrote this. Just under 36 hours later around 7:15 on Friday morning, I played the song Hallelujah, while driving to work. I started tearing up, but within seconds I began crying and then sobbing. I was crying so hard, and feeling so much warmth, I had to plead for it to stop. I told God I believed, and knew he was there, but I cannot keep sobbing or I will wreck my jeep... and like that I was able to calm down and finish my commute.

The experience was absolutely incredible. I had never tried anything quite like it. I urge you to try it for yourself. It may be the life changing experience you are looking for. I tried this experiment a second time, about a month later. The second time, we had responded to a vehicle that crashed into a fire hydrant, and our probie went to grab a shovel because there was a dirt mound preventing the door of the vehicle from opening. As the probie went to find the shovel, we were able to extract the patient. In the fire service, we relish the opportunity to have a little fun at the new guy's expense, so we did not tell him that the patient was out. We wanted him to come back with the shovel before we did so. Once we extricated the patient, our probie put the shovel back in the truck compartment and we drove back to the station. After backing the truck in the station, I stepped out of the truck and noticed he had left a Halligan sitting on the steel plated ledge of the truck, pick side down. It was sitting peacefully, as if waiting to be placed back in the truck. As a forcible entry tool that weighs around twelve pounds, if it had fallen off the truck, it could have caused some major carnage. Impressive that after a ten-minute drive, with copious amounts of turns and stop lights, the tool did not fall. Although more subtle perhaps, I took this as the sign I was looking for.

I have personally manifested many great things in my life. When I was working, prior to opening the Jiu-Jitsu studio, I had started to focus my thoughts on health and wealth. Before long, I felt a powerful drive to quit my job and open the studio. The job at the time was for a smaller Fire Department with less advancement opportunities. Also, we only averaged three to four calls a day, in the entire city, and I was used to a department with a much larger call volume. I remember a friend thought I was mad to quit my job with security and benefits for a front row seat to the unknown, and another friend asked, wasn't there already a Jiu-Jitsu place in the same city? I said yup, there were three other gyms within 20 minutes of us, but there were also many fast-food places and restaurants; so why couldn't there be more martial arts gyms? You see, like clockwork, fear and negativity were the common responses from others.

It would be a full year before I would return to the bigger fire department where I got my start in the field seven years earlier. After being without "traditional" employment for around six months, I reached out to the chief at training. He told me I was welcomed back anytime, so I took six more months to generate momentum at my gym before reentering the fire service. This too is testimony to good decisions and the law of attraction. Professional firefighting is a dream job and an amazing gig. You get to see behind the yellow tape, help the public and only work ten days a month with full benefits and good pay. Most people will either never make it into a department or will have to apply many times to get their shot, and here I was able to name my return date...and six months in advance. To say I am grateful is an understatement.

I never go a day without thanking God and the universe for life's many blessings, and I have thanked this chief personally, many times over. I found success because I refused to focus on lack or what I didn't want, and I did not let fear drive me. I have manifested so many great things in my life.

During the shutdown, my youngest son was having difficulty with being home every day and began feeling anxious, and so the idea of a dog came into our minds. We wanted a dog to bring a buddy into the home to cheer everyone up. At the time, our studio was shut down (we did not charge our students during the shutdown), so I only had the fire salary to pay our bills. We had an expensive taste in dogs, as we were interested in a bulldog. Within a couple days of deciding we would look for a dog, I began to envision and feel what it would be like to have a bulldog at home. The next morning, I was using the internet to search for bulldogs in for-sale ads and stumbled across a white ten-month-old bulldog. He was amazing, and only $700 instead of $2500-4000, which was what puppies were going for. Also, the woman that was selling him was under two hours' drive from the house. When we arrived at his residence, he was outside running around with a couple of children.

The owner said she was breeding the dogs, and the stud did not like him. Therefore, she had to get rid of him. It felt like an immediate cosmic connection, as the dog flopped over to show his belly, and allowed me to pick him up and whisk him away. Interestingly, for a few weeks after, he was a little bit aggressive to visitors, as we believe he was worried he would get taken from us on a whim, much like we took him. But he eventually understood this would not happen and settled into being a nice friendly house pet. He has been a wonderful addition to our family, and he and my son are best friends.

Also, during the shutdown, instead of hoarding toilet paper like the media addled masses, we purchased a brand-new Jet Ski (we live on the water, so it would be silly not to) and a new Toyota Tundra —my wife always wanted one. Everything I had read about the law of attraction stringently states you have to live abundantly if you want to receive abundance. You have to live and act as if what you want is already yours, sometimes literally. Obviously, this does not mean go out and purchase something that is going to tank you in debt, but if you can realistically wrap your head around affording whatever it is, go out and get it. I mention the purchases above, because if we had opted not to purchase said items, the decision would have been out of fear instead of faith.

We kept our gym closed from March to June because of the Virus, but then decided to reopen our doors. As we reopened, my wife had a great idea and created our intro program. From June to November, we added around 40 new students to the school. So, faith over fear won as we knew it would. We also aspire to be wealthy so we may help others.

This is another reason I aspire to be wealthy too. Helping others is one of my many long-term goals, and I have already begun providing help for others whenever my wallet or schedule allows. Prior to the 2020 madness, we had used our studio to hold two separate charity events, and we held one smaller event during the fall of 2020. Some people may be too prideful to accept help from family, but this is a lot like the metaphor about the woman stranded at sea that is asking God for help. God answered the call by sending boat after boat to help her, but she refused because she was waiting for "God" to help. The lady eventually died at sea because she was too proud or ignorant to receive the help that was given to her. The universe and God will use all the resources available to provide you with help and definitive leads, so do not make the mistake of thinking you have it all figured out. The law of attraction will always find a way to give you what you want, but you have to exude faith and do your part.

*"God helps those who help themselves."*

—ATTRIBUTED TO BEN FRANKLIN

You have everything in your life now to manifest your dreams, you just have to create the reality you want by your dominant thought patterns. You see the beauty of the law of attraction is you are utilizing energy and nature to create your reality. Something as simple as your diet and your body type, you can control with your thoughts. I read this and decided to try it. I have always stayed in the weight room and have been on the Jiu-Jitsu Tatami since my twenties. But I had a slight belly and was around ten pounds overweight in my early thirties. During the shutdown, I wanted to try to look more like Brad Pitt in Snatch, so I took to eating vegetables and fish only. I noticed my inflammation went away, I had more energy, and I perspired a lot less. I lost weight and did end up looking sinewy like Pitt. I did eventually add meat back into my diet (I purchased grass fed beef from a friend) and was able to add a few needed pounds. My point is, I did match the appearance that I held in my mind.

You see so many people believe they are destined to be overweight or have slow metabolism or be this or that —they believe it, and now you have magazines trying to convince women that being the size where hypertension and diabetes begins to be a problem is healthy, or that was what a recent cover was portraying to be true. But the most successful fitness models understand and always speak of the mind body connection. They understand the secret and are telling you that in order to achieve greatness, you have to believe it and connect your thoughts with your actions.

The three quickest reads I have found on the subject are *The Science of Getting Rich by Wallace Wattles, As a Man Thinketh by James Allen and It Works by RHJ.* For the past two years, I have stayed away from television, curtailed my use of social media and focused on imbibing as much law of attraction information as possible. Again, Einstein understood the law of attraction through the law of vibration, as he was not some singular genius that our schoolteachers and modern consensus would have us believe. Scholastically speaking, he was a complete failure. In reality, he was a man that was willing to question everything, and that led him to the laws of vibration and physics. If you decide to change your life, the greatest strategy I can paraphrase for you is to make a list. Write down your wishes on a piece of paper. Make sure these wishes cause no harm and do not compete with others... meaning have pure intentions, and utility in mind.

For example, I wouldn't say I want more students than so and so, or I want a better car than someone else. The universe will not grant these wishes (though Satan might, but you will pay for this eventually), but you are also wishing from lack. For that matter, do not ask in the negative. The universe and God understand the language of feeling more than words. Imagine trying to understand the nuances of every language that exists on this planet; instead, the universal consciousness understands our language by the feelings and emotions we assign to it. Plus, feelings and emotions equate to energy, as emotion is energy in motion. Again, keep your aspirations clear and positive. So, do not ask for less of something you do not want. Instead use only positive subject matter. For instance, do not ask to be less poor, ask for financial abundance, and do not buy into the notion of lack. You do not have to compete for what is already created; for if you do this, as Wattles puts it, you are wishing from the competitive realm not the creative.

Remember, we are all creators. We are all connected to the superconscious mind of infinite intelligence. We were never meant to be a divided and cutthroat species, but that is how the devil and negative forces of the universe take our power. So, write your list. Look at the list morning, noon, and night. Stay positive. Anytime you have a negative thought, bring out your list and read it, so you can squash the negativity immediately. Attach feelings to it. Your manifesting powers will work when you are able to feel as if you already have what is on your list. Hold no doubts. I highly recommend reading and implementing all the practices mentioned in *Think and Grow Rich*. Motivational speaker and wealth coach, Bob Proctor says he studies this book every day, and the book is good enough and replete with information to demand such a high level of study.

Also, try to stay consistent to maintain forward momentum with your desires. To paraphrase *Abraham Hicks* in the book *The Law of Attraction*, if you begin going in one direction, and then go in the opposite, and repeat this cycle on and on, you will never get where you originally set out to go. Our thoughts act this way too. If you begin strong, but then doubt yourself, you will halt progress and begin traversing in the opposite direction of your desires. The experience, in the beginning, will most likely be uncomfortable, as changing or creating anything major in your life will most likely require a rebirth.

In the book *Becoming Supernatural by Joe Dispenza,* he provides a great example of this when he talks about his friend who was the vice president of a university and was fired three weeks after beginning his meditations. He was the backbone of the university, so the firing seemed extreme and left him feeling uneasy. Dispenza encouraged him by telling him to let go of the feelings of survival to ensure he would not resort to living in the past and keep finding the present moment to continue creating his new future.

Within two weeks of his departure from the university, he fell in love with a woman who he later married. He received an offer for a better job as vice president of a much bigger university, which he accepted, and a year later the college that fired him asked him to return as president. Dispenza closes this example with a beautifully worded statement about the unknown, and how embracing it has always proved to be a valuable endeavor.

I couldn't agree more, as this is exactly how my life unfolded. Just prior to my resignation from the small department, I could not shake the feeling of needing more. I literally quit mid-day (even my wife was a little surprised when I came home mid-day) and turned in all my gear and equipment with courage and faith the universe would deliver on the feelings I had in my heart, mind and gut; it did deliver, above and beyond, and I have no regrets.

Think of attracting your dream life as planting seeds. If you deprive seeds of anything they need, they will not yield the results they are meant to. You have to plant the seeds (your thoughts) in good soil (your mind).

You then have to water the seed and give them plenty of sunlight (positive thoughts, beliefs and affirmations). Soon the seeds will yield whatever harvest you planted (goals and wishes). This happens in the fields of life, and it will happen in the field of your mind, but you have to believe and keep moving forward. Too often we plant these seeds, we see results, and then we sense or experience a plateau and quickly lose traction...ie, we quit watering them, so our aspirations wither and die.

Most people then give up and back track, often believing their first taste of success to be luck and nothing more. Or they become scared and worried at the first sign of trouble. Often, this is why people will become rich only to subsequently lose their fortunes. Somewhere along the way, they become doubtful and then afraid they will lose their money, and so they bring the opposite of what they want into existence. Make sure your desires remain positive too. For example, never say I don't want to be poor. You are saying the keyword poor and thinking from lack, so you will draw this to you. Instead, promote thoughts of wealth, such as "I am wealthy". It is important to always use the positive of whatever your dreams are when communicating with the universe and divine spirit. So, stay positive and do not allow doubts to enter your mind.

Just last night I was doubting the quality of my chapter about money and asked the universe for help. So, I was inspired to reread Wattles book *The Science of Getting Rich,* and arbitrarily worked with a guy from a different station and shift than me. I had never worked with this firefighter before and did not know he was into deeper level esoteric study like I was. We talked for about two hours, and I eventually mentioned my book. He offered some great ideas, and I was able to confidently revamp the chapter. Just like that, the universe answered the call. Another, similar, moment occurred during the editing phase of the ignominy chapter.

Do not worry about how the manifesting process will take shape. Believe the universe will set this up for you. At first it may seem strange to believe, but that's because we've all been programmed to believe no one is special and to rely only on the physical three-dimensional world. We have not been taught or encouraged to internally search for ways to improve ourselves.

In a consumerist world, they have a pill of placebo for everything, but we are capable of so much more than we believe or have been told to believe. We are the highest and most intelligent creation on this planet, yet we are the only species that is uncomfortable in our own environment, and where a majority of us rely on outside influence to feel adequate or alive. This is not normal, but we have accepted it as such.

Our thoughts create energy and disperse a wavelength that's undetectable to our senses. Because of the photons of light and what our eyes can actually perceive, we see less than one percent of what's really in our world. We can only see light waves that are part of the rainbow and between 400 and 700 nm. However, we cannot see the electromagnetic waves on the frequency of microwaves, or X rays, or signals from our phones or many other devices that transmit these waves, but we are able to enjoy the comforts of all the above and have no problem believing they exist.

We were never taught to think and utilize the power of our thoughts, but the universe will make your wishes a reality if you keep your thoughts focused. You can choose to stay with the masses, and believe the world is a mess and we have no control over anything, or you can start taking control of your life and create your dream life.

The other great thing about understanding and utilizing the law of attraction is you will have less room and desire in your life for drama and waste. Because you understand you are the gatekeeper to your happiness, you will suddenly see how dependent and broken most of society really is, and therefore you will be less likely to be swayed and controlled by the power of suggestive reasoning.

At the end of the day, if you are one of the many souls walking around feeling subdued and despondent, you have no one to blame but yourself. Even because of the 2020 Virus, the Governor isn't going house to house with a gun or machete and forcing his draconian mandates regarding masks; the police are not and cannot enforce these things. People choose their own prisons, and the machine knows this and needs this to be true. They do not have the numbers to truly narcotize and police society, and by nature, they cannot break natural law either. We have to choose to be docile and subservient;

this was true even before the pandemic. I have chosen to remain calm and cheerful because I was given the right by God. Jesus himself even came to the planet to show us the way. Stay positive and you will achieve great things. Life is good, and I hope you find your happiness.

# CHAPTER THREE: RESILIENCE

*"Success is not final, failure is not fatal,
it is the courage to continue that counts."*

—WINSTON CHURCHILL

There is an old saying, "no pressure, no diamonds", and yet another, "God tests us with stress before he trusts us with success". Without suffering, we will never comprehend and appreciate the beauty and accomplishments in our lifetime. Another great axiom is "when they say no, you say next", which helps to cultivate that no quit attitude.

Resilience is losing over fifteen percent of your gym members in two weeks (just before the holidays and after eight months of the Virus) and saying, "I'm good!" because you know there will be more joining members to come, and you refuse to let negativity and the fear of loss win. But wait, that is not all! Then you wake up the next day to yet another cancellation and then receive a phone call from a close friend that another friend and mutual acquaintance just got arrested for possession and distribution of child porn. You really respect this person, or use to respect him rather, as he has a wife, three kids and always portrayed himself as one of the good ones. Also, he is supposed to be a professional in a career in which the public still believes is the job that represents the pinnacle of manhood. I've got news for you, it should.

This shit happened on Dec 1, 2020. Up until this point, the year had been relatively normal, if not successful, considering most people bought into the idea that they were going to catch the Virus and die. Then the gates of Hell opened and released the kraken that is reality. I am not going to lie, knowing personally that a 16 year old girl of a Chaplain was fighting cancer, a close friend and coworker had just lost his mother in law to cancer, a few other friends had family members suffering from cancer treatments, another great friend and student had a son who was suffering from a terminal disease called Krabbe, and Virginia was refusing to enact a law that could screen for and prevent the disease, having 18 students quit in about two weeks and finding out a friend (who was married with three young children) was caught with and admitted to having child pornography, almost broke me —it all felt like too much.

Also, three of our members (a coach included) had caught the Virus the week prior (their symptoms were mild like a cold mind you), so this, a new tattoo, and the holiday had kept me from the mats for over two weeks; the mats are my therapy, and when I cannot go to therapy, I suffer. I have never needed to take pills or seek the company of a therapist, but I cannot live without the jiu-jitsu tatami. Once you have been part of a fight club, your life is not the same without it.

The day after I found out about my friend's disgusting and detestable habits on the internet, I went to the fire station for my first shift of that cycle. Me and another guy, who had known the accused for over nine years, couldn't shake the feelings of doom and gloom. So, we took the day off from work. We absolutely needed a mental health day, as we were on the medic that shift, and when your mind isn't right, the medic can be a dangerous place to be. I spent the day talking with my wife and hanging out with my kids and bull-dog. We wrapped up the evening by watching the Notebook (that movie is great by the way) and woke up the next day feeling invincible again...this my friends is resilience.

As for losing some students and money, resilience is taking it a step further, and scheduling a paint job the next week to regain every soon to be dollar lost, and almost to the exact penny. My wife is an absolute rock star by the way, as she sold the job.

I was forced to utilize resilience after taking a bad wrestling shot at one of our Saturday open mats. A few of us were practicing takedowns, as we have many former wrestlers as students. Earlier, I had thrown one of my students that was still in his twenties and over 300 pounds —this young man is 300 pounds and highly mobile. Our next round I attempted a double leg takedown but fell in pain as he sprawled all his weight on me. I laid on the mats for about a good minute then got up and finished the round. I was able to defensively win the round but could feel my left shoulder was possibly injured (I thought I had heard a pop too during the shot). The rest of the day my mobility was hindered, and I felt intense discomfort in that scapula area of my left arm. I also utilized Ice to help quell any swelling (To put into perspective. I have been grappling since my early twenties and have only needed ice three times). The next morning, I had maybe five percent mobility in my left arm. For example, I could not raise my arm to put my shirt on and could not use my left hand to raise a drink to my mouth. Instead of assuming the worst, I meditated and communicated with the creator that with his help, I would be twenty five percent better at day's end. Against my wife's advice, I worked out in the garage with what little I could do and washed my truck. By the next day, I had over twenty five percent mobility again. The thought of surgery or torn anything did not cross my mind, unlike anytime others (typically younger than me) have moments where pops are heard, and pain/ discomfort ensues. I chose mind over matter and allowed the stored energy within my mind and body to heal me from within. Now, roughly two months later, I am learning more about mobility by using bands and bodyweight exercises and have more mobility than before.

An even better example of resilience is a child, of about 12 years old that has a rare disease that stunts his growth and gives him digestion problems. So, this child is quite small compared to other lads his age. This 12-year-old is relegated to the hospital for around six months with hopes of an improvement in his condition, and every time his mother checks on him, though he's extremely haggard, tired and worn down from ongoing tests and lack of sleep, he gives a thumbs up and a smile, no matter how hopeless his day is. You see, because this little warrior cannot bear to see his mother upset or worried, he will fight with every fiber of his being to be sure she maintains her smile. In reality, most cannot fathom how bad his days actually are. I spent many moments praying for this guy and was absolutely ecstatic when I found out he came home. I have met many grown men who would cower and crumble at the pain and suffering the little warrior endured (I have lost count of how many grown "Men" shriek in pain when receiving an IV on the medic), yet he kept trucking and eventually won the fight.

One last example is the kid referenced in Forrest Griffin's book, *Got Fight*. In the book, they chose to pick on a kid that appeared weak and frail. The episode ended with one of Forrest's friends throwing the kid down a hill, because no matter what they did, the kid kept coming back to defend his honor; he was willing to fight to the death. Most of us know the archetype of the tough kid that will fight you to the death, even though that same kid weighs 120lbs soaking wet and looks like a character from Revenge of the Nerds, hence why you don't provoke fights with strangers half your size, or anyone really.

Most bullies just want to get a free shove or slap out of an altercation, but you never know how deep the fighting spirit goes in other people.

I witnessed two situations, early in life, where a friend was the bully, but the guys he bullied were way more badass and crazier than he was. Both occurred in middle school. One was in the bathroom; he grabbed a nerdy (I don't agree with this term, but this was the middle school thought of mind) kid and began kneeing the life out of him. It looked exactly like the *Anderson Silva vs. Rich Franklin* fight, only in this scenario, Rich was a spectator and not a trained fighter. The kid I guess was a little lippy before the blows but did not warrant the flurry of knees. The kid ended up with a quick swollen cheek and black eye. My buddy realized the weight of what he had just done and started apologizing in a panic.

The kid leaned over the trash can, spit out some blood, and said "I ain't no NARC". The kid then threw on his backpack and limped out of the bathroom as if nothing had happened, and he wasn't kidding about keeping his mouth shut. The moment was never spoken of again, and my buddy never contemplated laying a hand on the kid either.

Another situation was at a friend's house in middle school, and a buddy began slapping our friend's younger brother. The younger brother was quiet, and pretty much kept to himself, so my buddy assumed he was easy prey. The younger brother did not take kindly to the slaps, and in a rage grabbed a hammer and started swinging it at my buddy while grunting like the waterboy during a tackle. Luckily, my buddy used his forearms to block the hammer, and ran outside until the little brother calmed down. As quickly as it happened, the situation dissipated. This too was never spoken of again. Resilience isn't always about how you deal with bullies, but it goes to show that you do not have to be big, strong and macho to display great resilience. Sadly, today there appears to be a lack of resilience in our society.

Just recently, we had a young man attend one of our intro classes, offered by our jiu-jitsu studio. He could not make it through the warm up without stopping to show a great display of injury. The first night he was rubbing his knee and complaining of severe pain under five minutes into class. The second class he complained about his asthma and elbow pain. As a forty-year-old man that can still wrestle with youthful giants, I did not pander or placate this young man. My wife, who is in her forties, is quite often my Uke. Which means I use her to show technique, and she never complains. With this young man, I was kind, but I did not encourage his behavior. After his four intro classes, we never saw him on the mats again.

Maybe it all began with the elimination of dodgeball, monkey bars and merry-go-rounds in schools, or the disparaging of bullies. Don't get me wrong, I loathe bullies, but I also understand their place in society. In a way our thoughts can be seen as our friends or our mental bullies.

Anytime, your day is derailed by negativity or loathful thinking, are you not struggling to rise up against the unwanted thinking? It goes back to the saying, misery loves company. Negative thinking snowballs and grows with time as if you have an entire gang of bad apples living in your own head. Next time you converse with a negative person, pay attention to the laundry list of complaints they offer about life —it's quite staggering and depressing.

I have also met some really cool people that truly believe that they cannot win in life, and there is always something negative waiting for them around the corner. I do my best when conversing with them, to point out the positives, but this is something we all have to figure out on our own. Overcoming any adversity always starts with the reflection in the mirror. Another real example of bullies involved my son and an interaction he was having in middle school. My son was getting bullied in school, in the sixth grade, so I gave him the green light to knock the bullies block off. He did, and the bullying ceased. It could be debated that trying to prevent and protect our kids from ever experiencing bullies in their youth (with the zero-tolerance bullying movement) is what is actually toxic.

You see, the bully is a real scenario. I have seen it countless times in my adult years; in fact, when I was still a probie in the fire department, and a purple belt in jiu-jitsu, two firefighters that outweighed me approached me in the locker room. They were being playful and physical, but they had just tried to put another, much older firefighter in a small metal locker. I have a rule: I will never touch or start anything with you, but if you come at me, it's game on. As a shy person, I do not enjoy pretend fighting and never have; it always escalates with me. So, I choked the life out of both of them, multiple times, and at the same time. Don't believe me, ask around the fire department, and you will see; that moment was shared and talked about for a long time after. Had I not known how to defend myself and physically handle that situation, I really do not know how it would have ended —probably not well.

When I was young and in elementary school, there were moments where I was bullied and did nothing to stop or prevent it, and the experience haunted me for a very long time. There were also times in my early twenties, where I had interactions with rude people, and regretted not practicing a little social karate. It also goes back to the big three, be kind, be humble, be ready. When any scenario tries to break you, you need to be ready. Bullies are one of those scenarios, and even if you have no idea how to fight, standing up to one is a life changing event, and will be a lasting memory for those involved. I would venture to think those experiences will also generate the feeling of moxy and resilience, which every man should have a healthy supply of.

With the extinction of bullies, we are depriving future men of victories early in their childhood. During most of my time on the medic, one of the most common maladies we responded to was anxiety, and quite often from men. Because of anxiety, the patients would be mirroring symptoms of a heart attack or sometimes a complete mental breakdown, which is actually because they were in what's called a high-frequency beta wave state; in fact, once we were able to rule out the major stuff, most of the time we could trace it back to anxiety. We have a plethora of magical, medical equipment on the medic that we can use to take a diagnostic look at a person's vital signs and heart rhythm. Again, this helps us rule out the really bad stuff, like an actual myocardial infarction or TIA —though we can only make suggestions of our best guess based on our findings in the field.

Just the other day I was speaking to a relative about them having ulcers and anxiety, and he proceeded to tell me I did not understand, and that he could not help suffering from these infirmities. I tried to explain that actions, thoughts and beliefs are what caused his anxiety, not the world around him, but he wasn't having it. Convincing people against their beliefs is a tall order, and I do not like to spend my time doing so; but I often offer a quick suggestion of positive thinking and leave it at that.

*Edward Bernays* explains in great detail in his book, *Propaganda,* that once minds are regimented and made up, it is incredibly or nearly impossible to change them. Also, *Napoleon Hill,* or the devil rather, in *Outwitting the Devil,* calls this mode of stuck thinking or action, "hypnotic rhythm". Basically put, once people have made up their minds about themselves or done things a certain way for so long, it takes a conscious and strenuous effort to change. Otherwise, they succumb to their habits; according to *Hill,* 98 percent of society will remain stuck in their thinking and actions. Recognizing and initiating change is no small endeavor for anyone. This is also the crux of what Resilience really is —the willingness to accept something as faulty and make an effort for change, no matter how uncomfortable the process.

So, why are so many people affected by anxiety and believe they have no control over it? I believe as a society, we have been convinced that we are all victims of circumstance, and we have no control over what happens to us. We are not taught how to internally fix or repair the pitfalls of our lives, as they have a drug or external placebo for just about everything. Basically, normal behavior for most is if you have too many off days, you can take medication to help curtail those days. The news does a great job of convincing us the world is a terrible place to live, and we are all slaves to bad news. On my worst days, I may even buy into this a little bit, but having resilience is also what combats the anxiety from getting a foothold. You could call it optimism or positivity, but I wonder why we are not being brainwashed as a society to see the beauty in the world?

Why are we slowly removing, not religion (as I care not about man made dogma), but God from anything and everything related to society. I mean, a friend of mine whose son is 12, has told me that he is an atheist. At 12! I didn't even know what that was at 12, and I certainly wouldn't have written God off entirely by then either.

It actually makes sense if you do not believe in a certain god, or Christ specifically, but to truly believe this all just happened because of a random boom in the cosmos —it does not quite add up. The only reaction that is a given after a large explosion is chaos and disorder, not the opposite. If I really believed in nothing beyond myself, and there was no purpose for any of us being here, I too would be a mess, and would require someone with a degree, and the power to prescribe controlled substances, to absolve me of my perceived problems. Another possibility is we have it all wrong.

God does not want us to hurt or suffer, as many would have us believe. But God speaks and listens to feelings and will allow our feelings to mirror our reality. The word "resilience" should not even be a part of our lexicon, as hardships and difficult times are not something that is natural or necessary, but we humans have brought suffering to be. There are many books on this, and I suggest reading *The Divine Matrix by Gregg Braden*, as he mixes science and spirituality in an easily read format, and early on in his book he discloses that substituting the virtual over the real world can hinder our ability to live rich and meaningful lives. He also makes that statement, with the lack of resilience and internal moxy, people will find a crutch to ease the burdens of life, apparently through all the technology available to society.

As for speaking of God, we are all connected via the superconscious mind or unified field of energy. We are not told this in religion, but we have a direct line to God to ask for anything or any help we could ever need. The rub is we have to believe it. We cannot ask in desperation, as desperation shows no faith in the forthcoming miracles and wishes. We have to believe the help is happening, almost to the level of expecting it. And as Descartes says, "I think therefore I am", Which many thinkers agree we know we have consciousness. To go further, our reality is a reflection of our thoughts and beliefs. So, no matter what the day throws at me, I know my internal reaction dictates the true reality of the situation. I am not in complete agreement with *Abraham Hicks* or any law of attraction royalty, on the idea that we bring about every circumstance to our reality, as sometimes some really gnarly shit just happens; I could not be convinced that my friend's (who was proven to be a pedophile) wife brought on the ramifications of her husband's actions, based on her dominant thoughts.

I could be convinced that she brought on some of the reality because she married the guy, but that could mean that every person who ever marries anyone is entitled to enduring such hardship; that does not sit right. She too, assuming she makes it out of their situation with her wits intact, could write a book on resilience.

In Bob Proctor's book, *The Art of Living*, he references another great writer, Michael Beckwith by stating three things. Number one, it is what it is. Sometimes stuff happens (the bible is loaded with "stuff happens" moments), and as Rocky Balboa's eponymous saying goes, "it is what it is".

Number two, harvest the good or find the good in anything and everything. For example, when dealing with other people perhaps instead of saying I don't like that person, you could frame your opinion differently by saying I do not understand them. This way, you are still trying to glean the good. Thinking negative about others does no harm to them, but causes plenty of harm to you; it only steals from your positive energy.

Number three, forgive all the rest...just let it be. So basically, negative things just happen —get over it. Stay positive and focus on the good and let everything else go; talk about being absolutely spot on.

Another example of how stuff sometimes just happens, I was looking under the hood of my truck and a rodent decided to make his home under there. It was early winter, so he was searching for somewhere warm to survive. He had a grand time chewing wires and tearing up the hood insulation. I take pride in my truck and wash and spray wax it just about every few weeks. I am not sure my thoughts could have manifested a little creature to wreak havoc in my engine compartment. But I do have a choice of how to handle the aftermath of the situation, and I chose to clean up after the bugger and take it to the dealership to ensure I did not miss anything that needed replacing. This is not unlike the flat tire situation that most of us have had to endure on more than one occasion. We cannot change the circumstances when this happens, but we get to choose how we handle the situation with our attitude and actions.

A great excerpt from a timeless masterpiece of a book talks about our thoughts in relation to our reality; *James Allen* via *As a Man Thinketh,* states that basically our circumstances mirror our thinking. I have been practicing law of attraction for over three years, and when I can actually conjure the feeling of receiving, I have been able to attract amazing experiences quickly into my life. Interestingly, it almost seems the more good and enjoyment I attract into my life, the harder Satan works to try and ensnare me against it. Resilience is knowing what is happening and continuing the fight day in and day out.

Most people will allow the negative days to stymie their forward progress; just look at all the negative reviews for new thought books. People are so quick to form an opinion, look for gaps or holes in the pages, and focus on all of their negative circumstances. This is not resilience. I do feel if you are currently alive, despite what the media and general consensus is of the public, you hit the cosmic lottery. Just today I was thinking I have perfect vision, perfect sense of smell, taste. I can hear, read and write. I can walk without a cane or crutch, and I can think on my own. There is so much to be thankful for.

I worked with another crew this morning, and one of the crew men had recently been in a collapsed floor situation during a live fire. He, and three other firefighters were temporarily trapped and eventually made it out alive, and with a few bruises and light burns to boot. I can only assume these phenomenal men, obviously resilient, resembled the guy in the film Fight Club, who had a gun pointed to his head by Brad Pitt's character, but was allowed to live. The food they were able to taste the next day probably tasted the best it had ever tasted, and even though it was raining outside, the world never seemed brighter; their perspective had been replaced with optimum levels of gratitude for life because their life had been spared; it was a near death experience. But it should not take a near death experience for us to experience the beauty of life that is all around us. We have been sent here to help raise the vibration of the planet and provide good in some way, and the only way to experience this amazing journey is to actually be here.

Despite the ephemeral "off" days, I am constantly looking at the world around me, and the life I have created, and cannot help but be shrouded in complete and utter gratitude. I am blessed and grateful to know that my thoughts, beliefs, choices and actions dictate my reality. I am grateful that free will is the hand that holds the brush to paint my entire reality and exis-tence, and I vow "to keep moving forward, opening new doors and doing new things", as recommended by Walt Disney, no matter what vicissitudes of fortune may try to befall me.

Although terrible things will keep occurring in the world around us, as History proves this a truism, we will always have the power to continue in our journey with confidence, joy and positivity. And with enough practice, the journey will become easier and more enjoyable with the hope that someday we will all be able to pass on knowledge of life's journey to our future brothers and sisters that walk the planet earth. Lastly, if you like to pray, please pray with conviction and belief. Do not pray in desperation or despair, as this will be how your reality is returned to you. Pray like you know your prayers will be answered, and miracles will follow you. Remaining steadfast and resilient in your endeavors and life will be the rewarding experience it was meant to be.

# CHAPTER FOUR: JIU-JITSU (THE GENTLE ART)

*"Our fears don't stop death, they stop life."*

—RICKSON GRACIE

What I cherish most about jiu-jitsu, is it is the ultimate noise and distraction cancelling device. This week alone, they cancelled a show called *Calliou* because the main character got into too much mischief, and the show did not offer enough diversity in gender and race. There is a new children's show in Denmark titled, *John Dillermand*, about a middle-aged man that cannot control his incredibly long penis (and he resembles the infamous porn legend Ron Jeremy), and there was a coup to rattle the cages of our government by the so called rowdy Republicans. If I could not find a way to cancel the noise that Satan and the evil forces of the world were so desperately trying to pervade us with, I too would most likely succumb to this so-called reality and turn to one of any vices available to quell the noise; thankfully I have jiu-jitsu. Clearly some level of stress in life is inevitable, but with jiu-jitsu, this is what's called hormetic stress (or mid-frequency beta waves), and this is good.

"Be Kind, Be Humble, Be Ready!" This is our motto, in order of importance at our jiu-jitsu studio. Sometimes the first two actions are not enough, and you have to stand your ground or teach an unfortunate lesson, and when this happens, you better be ready.

If you think real Jiu-Jitu is anything remotely close to the action that was in that Nicholas Cage movie, think again. Movies like that were cool in the 80s. Trust me I know. I would have been in heaven with that movie, when I was seven. Just watching the trailer gave me a head and stomach ache. Too bad, with a moniker like Jiu-Jitsu, any movie could have been pure gold at the box office. There is however a movie called *Born a Champion*, starring actual black belt in jiu-jitsu, *Sean Patrick Flannery*, that is really good. As for real Jiu-Jitsu, my journey began like this.

Growing up as a pipsqueak, I wanted to be a ninja so bad. I loved kung fu movies, Bruce Lee and ninja turtles. I would spend hours in my front yard practicing karate and katas. I would challenge my friends to kumite matches. I even studied karate, Kenpo to be exact, for a few years. Skateboarding was my ultimate love during my early teen years, so over time I lost interest in the martial arts until I was in my early twenties.

As for my first real jiu-jitsu experience, there I was, an ex-high school wrestler at around twenty-four years old. I was around 200 pounds of gym hardened mass, and the ego to go with it. I was training (more like floundering) with a blue belt student, who was around 150 pounds, and he choked me about twenty times in two minutes.

I desperately tried to dish out the same medicine but came up short with not one single win or point scored. I felt completely and utterly helpless against a guy much smaller than me. I was also very sloppy and choppy with my movements, as he was smooth and calm. I even accidentally kicked my partner a few times while trying to mimic the chokes that he had just done to me. He made me pay for this blunder. I was completely flabbergasted and out of my element and could not believe the reality of the situation; but I was also instantly hooked. Looking around the room and seeing all the varying belt colors and degrees, I understood the gravity of the situation, and knew right then, I would be a black belt someday. At this time, there were not many black belts in the states, and especially not in the Southern Maryland area.

Being able to train with anyone who had a purple belt or higher was a rarity at this time.

Prior to this day, I had only been able to imbibe jiu jitsu through books and Pride FC. Most people had not heard of jiu-jitsu at this time, or not understood it. My parents had cable, so I was always excited to hang with them and catch a fight at their house. I remember watching the Gracies in early UFC days and Pride and being amazed at what they could do...fighting from their backs and winning; it was amazing to see. I had purchased a bjj book from the bookstore, and began doing mental reps instantly. Attending college at this time, I vividly remember asking one of my buddies to attack me. We were outside our dorm when he lunged at me, and I quickly pulled guard and grabbed his arm for a kimura, which is a shoulder lock. I had just done mental reps the day before by studying the pictures in the book. He tapped, and I felt the first big rush of joy —I had actually done Jiu-Jitsu! Also, whenever I would rough house with my friends, I would typically be victorious from my previous wrestling experience.

Naturally, I thought I would jump right into the mid to upper-level ranks at a bjj school, but this was absolutely not reality. Other white belts were wiping the floor with me, during my first six months of practice. Jiu-Jitsu is the real deal, and no matter how macho people think they are, technique and mat time always wins. My first exposure to the art was at a Loyd Irvin school, but after completing a month of introductory exposure, the distance from my house proved too much for me to endure. Not long after, a Relson Gracie school opened up about ten minutes from my house, and they were running the program out of the gym I had already been a member of. So, the place quickly felt like home. I stayed with the Relson school until moving South a year later, just after receiving my blue belt. Receiving my blue belt made me feel like an absolute badass, as this was a lofty achievement at the time, where bjj schools were difficult to come by and most professional MMA fighters were only blue belts.

When I relocated to Virginia, there were only two schools within a half hour of my house, and one was a nogi only school. So, I chose the other. The head instructor there was a brown belt. I would go on to receive my purple belt under the Gustavo Machado lineage and brown and black under Ribeiro. My journey from white to black belt was around eleven years. About six months after receiving my black belt, I decided I needed a change in my jiu-jitsu, so I joined the Jiu-Jitsu For Life Team with my buddy and black belt Alan; this meant our students could intermingle at open mats (although I never cared if my students went elsewhere to train, as long as the other place was clean. We have never had a skin infection outbreak at our place) and participate in the big tournaments hosted by IBJJF, which is like the NFL of jiu-jitsu tournaments. Also, Alan had always been laid back and kind to me, so I wanted to team up with someone who shared my energy and zest for life in general.

Since first discovering the gentle art, I have become a well-rounded, humble and confident man. If you have ever heard of Maslow's hierarchy of needs, or any basic psychological rhetoric, then you understand the importance of safety and self-preservation on our psyche. Knowing that most of the population cannot harm you (I am not talking with guns or knives of course, as that opens up another can of worms) is a freeing feeling and allows you to immediately remove a big hindrance, fear, from most of your life decisions. I have no problem looking men or women (haha), who are much bigger and meaner looking than me, in the face and telling them I do not fear you. This does not mean that I walk around with a chip on my shoulder... quite the opposite. My shoulders are relaxed, as am I. The statement of you cannot harm me is a strange thing to say to someone, but if someone more sizable than me were to ask, that would be my answer.

Prior to rejoining the larger fire department, a muscular guy that worked there, saw me in the gym with a fire department shirt on. He said, "Hey you can't wear that shirt." I playfully, yet seriously said in a challenging tone, "Are you going to make me take it off?" He said, "I am not going to make you do anything." That was that. *Helio Gracie*, one of the founders of jiu-jitsu, and a small man in stature, was known to playfully taunt much younger and bigger practitioners by telling them they had to beat him, not the other way around. This is certainly how it has played out for me.

I have sparred (rolled) with so many people, many younger and much bigger and stronger than me, and have yet to lose to anyone untrained in the art. I have grappled with many wrestlers, good wrestlers, and they too cannot overcome the technical advantage Jiu-Jitsu offers, assuming we are practicing jiu-jitsu. However, I also encourage and teach a good deal of wrestling, as supplementation to the art.

We once had a guy come into our studio that was much taller than me and jacked. He dwarfed even our biggest student at the time, and he made sure to don a cut off shirt to broadcast this fact too. He told us he did not have much experience, and then while rolling, he began to lay waste to my white belts. The mats were adorned with a slew of bodies as if an actual pandemic had just taken place. He even forced one of my good white belts to tap to an ankle lock. This was interesting because we had only been open around ten months at the time. For those who do not know this, leg locks were considered taboo not too long ago in the art because they were not well studied or understood. Recently, the top level nogi competitors in the world use them regularly and dominate the sport because of them. We however teach and understand leg locks very well at our school, but to have a visitor best one of our white belts by one, is impressive.

So, I rolled with this giant and caught him in a triangle. He jerked out of it so hard, and somehow fell backwards onto my big toe. I instantly knew my toe was broken, so then I dialed my pressure way up. As I mounted him and covered his face with my lapel (I do this to cook my opponent by making them re-breathe their own $CO_2$ and tire them), he began to thrash and become claustrophobic. Under my weight while trying to breathe, in a muffled voice, he then asked me if I treated all my guests this way. I said nope, but I am teaching you a lesson. I later found out that his father practiced Jiu-Jitsu and he had stated he had over 1000 hours of mat time. This is not what he told us when he signed the waiver to try a free class. He never came back; I was fine with that.

After this encounter, we never allowed visitors to roll with our students until a coach or myself rolled with them first. We wanted to be sure to keep our students safe from sandbaggers who just wanted to hurt people or prove they were tough guys. Regarding those wanting to hurt people, I also agree with the statement "you cannot truly call yourself peaceful unless you are capable of causing great violence. If you are not capable of violence, you are not peaceful, you are harmless." Watch just about any video on the internet with real street fights, and you will see that most people are terrible at it. Even more, if you do see someone that has good hands and can move on their feet well, it is extremely rare they have a ground game. *Kimbo Slice* had amazing hands and proved he could do much damage when he used them, but he never acclimated all that well to grappling.

This is why Jiu-Jitsu is so powerful. Though we dabble in strikes (more so to defend strikes), we teach a plethora of takedowns, and spend hours upon hours sparring from the ground. Someone who is six foot four, is much shorter when they are forced to the ground and stuck on their back from your top pressure. I also liken the logic of Jiu-Jitsu to the boulder and pebble philosophy. If you place a small rock under a boulder in just the right spot, you can leverage the boulder to move —Jiu-Jitsu is no different. It's a game of leverage and technique. Strength helps, but as I have seen and experienced, it is not necessary.

Because of Jiu-Jitsu, little guys have been weaponized with ways to defeat bigger stronger guys. The world champion *Mikey Musumeci* and the *Miyao* brothers are but a few examples of this. Our art is considered human chess, and we who practice the art, have been likened to nerds because of the sheer volume of study entailed in the art. Many of my students get together and play Dungeons and Dragons, or collect comic books, and these people are absolute savages on the mat. Ryan Hall, who is currently in the UFC, and skinny, cannot get a fight. Because his Jiu-Jitsu is so good, he has caused many of the best to tap quickly to his submission game, and many opponents are not comfortable or willing to take a fight against him. There is also a video of Ryan taking a drunk man down (who was accosting him) in public and holding him down until police arrived. The drunk guy had it coming, but the video also displayed how applicable jiu-jitsu is in the real world to subdue instead of harm.

Jiu-Jitsu is however called the gentle art, as you do not employ strikes or typical means of attacking your opponent. Instead, Jiu-Jitsu teaches technique and leverage to grapple, sweep, submit or subdue your opponent. Since I began in the early/mid 2000s, the art has changed and advanced immensely, with sport jiu jitsu being the more popular avenue over self-defense application. It's absolutely brilliant how many ways you can choke or subdue your opponent with your kimono or theirs. Also, nogi (grappling in tight fitting clothes, so no grips on clothing allowed) is a second option of study in the art.

One of the more exciting guards, called the worm guard, is where you lock your opponent into a precarious position by using their gi. It's a combination of a different guard titled *De Lariva guard and lapel guard.* A well-known black belt named *Keenan Cornelius* created the position and coined the name. In 2019, my wife and I drove to Raleigh for his seminar, to learn the worm guard; It is literally one of many options of play, when practicing the art. Jiu-Jitsu is so functional and relevant to fighting as aforementioned, Ryan Hall, who is currently in the UFC cannot get a fight because his jiu jitsu is that good. His last few fights have ended quickly via leg lock. Garry Tonon is another BJJ maven on his way to this dilemma. Gary displayed amazing Jiu-Jitsu in his grappling only career and is doing great things in MMA.

Jiu Jitsu has changed my life. I walk tall and stand proud because at the end of the day, I know I won't take an ass whooping (or at least the odds are in my favor), and knowing that as a blue belt, my wife can defend herself and possibly best an assailant, allows me to rest much easier at night. The art has also shaped me into a kind and humble human being. I employ no ego when I talk with friends or strangers, and I have had my ego radar turned off for years; it's quite rare that I leave a conversation thinking that guy had a big ego. I believe your energy changes when you have a depth of knowledge regarding fighting; fighters live their lives on a different frequency, and I am not talking about assholes like War Machine, who is currently serving time for assault on a woman. People who do those things are the opposite of what a fighter should be, and they are absolutely not manly. They are just toxic.

I am speaking about the many good men and women that serve our country and are quiet snipers or the black belt that speaks kind and softly...

the type of person that does not need to exude a stentorian front to convince themselves or others they are tough.

Typically, the most dangerous and well-trained person in the room is the quietest and least assuming, and this is true of the jiu-jitsu mats. Jiu-Jitsu is great for men because it gives us an outlet for violence. Unfortunately, violence is in our DNA, and any history book will confirm this. The Jiu-Jitsu mats offer a safe, educational and fun way to learn self-defense, be around other great people and learn all the details of the art of violence. There is no way of knowing exactly how a bad situation will end when one occurs. Clearly the more practiced you are for the worst-case scenario, the better chance of survival. As a man, I feel it is our job to protect our family and household from whatever evils may come knocking at the door. If something were to happen to me, I would expect my sons to take over and protect their mother and our home. Both of my sons have been doing BJJ for years and understand how to shoot a gun safely.

It can be reasoned, the people who have phobias of guns are the people who know nothing about them and are content to allow others to make their decisions for them. Fighting is no different. Early on in the UFC years, the fights were seen as barbaric and the practitioners crazy. There had been a desire for a certain level of realism and barbarism, from the public, as ECW and other wrestling organizations were pushing the use of barbed wire, bats and other objects to wreak havoc on people's skulls and bodies. The UFC however, answered the call with real fighting and no rules whatsoever. The rules were obviously a bit lacking in the beginning, but now MMA is one of the most talked about and enjoyed entertainment options available.

Unlike most entertainment sports like football and baseball, anyone at any time can join a jiu-jitsu or MMA gym, where the best in the business practice, and learn what they are seeing on the television.

As for learning jiu-jitsu, the learning curve I tell most people to comprehend the bare basics is around six months; this is assuming you can train at least twice a week. For the lucky few that can train more often, they will advance quicker than most. It took me around 11 years to achieve the black belt, as I was working two jobs and raising kids during my journey.

Regarding where to train, there are a plethora of black belts all over the world now, so finding a school should not be too difficult. I tell people it's all about the vibe. I have seen so many good people become part of the jiu-jitsu social network. We are entrusting our lives to each other when we train and getting extremely close (literally) to one another. I consider the tatami my therapy, as do many others. So, make sure you like the vibe of the place that you choose.

Our school reopened in June of 2020, (after being closed for three months because of the virus) once we realized being closed was worse for the health and morale of our students, and originally the deal was to flatten the curve and not eradicate any cold like symptoms from the face of the earth. We did not make masks mandatory or litter our entryway with signs about masks but did take everyone's temperature at the front desk. It was the one place our students could go to feel normal and be around like-minded people. This was especially important for the youth students, as for most, this was the only tangible exercise they were getting. As for choosing a school, like receiving multiple estimates for home improvement, you should go and try a week at as many schools as possible and pick the one that feels right to you. I do not agree with some people's beliefs, that if you are not on the mats every day you are not dedicated, as most of my students have careers and a home life. Therefore, they have to come to some level of balance and time management with their training. However, I do agree if you want to be relevant in the competition world, you do have to make jiu-jitsu a main focus in your life.

Competing in jiu-jitsu is still one of the things that scares the shit out of me because my friends and sometimes family are watching, and the fear of failure is in the forefront of my thoughts. The inner demons and voices of inadequacy come out in droves to beat me down when I am competing. Typically, by the time my matches start, I am exhausted from worrying and dealing with the nerves all day. Some of my students deal with this type of performance anxiety as well. But this is also why I love competing, and recommend others compete. It is one of the few fears left I have to conquer. I am an introvert, yet public interaction, even in front of people, does not intimidate me. Responding to a bad medic or fire call does not get me too excited, but competing in BJJ, that is some scary stuff. But overcoming fear and getting better is part of the journey.

That is another great thing about Jiu-Jitsu, before the virus took over the world, you could sign up for a bjj competition (within driving distance) just about every other week, and my hope is that this will again be the norm. As a studio, we would attend a tournament every so often, and it was amazing to see our students compete and put their skills to the test. Competing isn't for the faint hearted, as not every school honors the proper belt and experience system.

One of our youth students, who had been training for about six months, competed against another kid that threw a flying armbar in under a minute. This led to my students' defeat, mentally and physically. Flying armbars are not a novice attack, but would venture to say an advanced attack, and my student had every right to be upset. Needless to say, it was a devastating experience for our student. I did my best to console him and told him how proud I was of him, but he was never the same. Subsequently, he quit his jiu-jitsu journey. I hope someday he will rejoin a jiu-jitsu gym, but for now the loss appears to be too much for him. Luckily this isn't the norm, as most matches are pretty fair and are typically won on heart and basics in the early years.

Competing is still the one demon I have yet to conquer, so there will unfortunately be more of it in my future. Please know many students consider their jiu-jitsu team their extended family. In fact, I am at the fire station editing this tonight, but there is a big gathering tonight (for all Breakaway students) to watch a UFC fight —and many will attend. Also, just recently, one of our incredibly generous students rented out a bourbon bar for Breakaway students, for the "Breakaway Bourbon" night. Because of the virus, attendance was limited to thirty-five people, and we filled the place to capacity. So, if you decide to give jiu-jitsu a try you will automatically gain a bunch of best friends, and it can be quite magical indeed.

# CHAPTER FIVE: HANDYMAN

*"If Wall Street can borrow money at 0.75% interest, so can college students. We need to stop treating students like profit centers."*

—ELIZABETH WARREN

*"The man who lives by his labor is at least free."*

—BENJAMIN FRANKLIN

To the above quote, there is a way to learn what needs to be learned and not become an indentured servant to the government in the process, join the trades and pay for your own college. In the trades, you become a real time understudy of those you work for, and as Hill talks about in the book *How to Own Your Own Mind,* you have a chance to attend *"the university of practical experience, and to receive good pay for the privilege."* Of course, he was speaking about the secretary field, but the message is the same. Thanks to technology, there would seem to be a large quantity of information out there about anything and everything, and because of the unending abundance of information, you would think anyone could pretty much do anything on their own these days. But you would be wrong, or perhaps partially right...I know what you are thinking, that was clear as mud yes.

Yes, there is no lack of youtube videos or books on any topic you can fathom, but there is simply too much saturation of information, and has been for years. Lack of guided hierarchy of information is the main problem. Also, when you go online or use youtube to teach yourself a trade, often ads or video suggestions will get the best of you, and eventually you forget why you went to the site in the first place. However, If you have the schedule and attention span to research these options for hours on end, then you can unearth some valuable information and practices. Also, if you utilize the 40/70 rule as recommended by Colin Powell and referenced in the book *Limitless* by *Jim Kwik*, where you gather about forty percent of available information and resources, but no more than seventy as a balance point, you can balance your research and time wisely to achieve exemplary results.

Generally speaking, it will always be faster, more efficient and safer to go straight to the source, as in an actual job site. The other problem is there is an abundance of erroneous information available as well. Being in the trades for so long, I have had many conversations with friends where they found something online, but it wasn't the best or even correct way to do the task they were interested in. Or the product suggestion was completely wrong but intended to sell a sponsor's product.

I still get calls or texts quite often from friends regarding painting trade secrets; the biggest question is always about priming. You cannot go wrong with oil-based primer, as it will adhere to just about every surface, and you can cover a plethora of unwanted stains with it. Exterior house washing was another hot topic. When I used to soft wash houses, my dad asked me what I used, as it cleaned the siding perfectly —it's exterior bleach and water by the way. Always rinse from the bottom up, and especially with aluminum siding or you will get streaks; this technique only requires the pressure of a garden hose. I would only soft wash about six to eight exteriors a year, so I kept it simple and mixed the solution with a two-gallon pump sprayer, but there are better and quicker ways to get the work done if you are inclined.

I got my start in the trades when I was going to college. I was working at Bob Evans as a cook and hated it. My girlfriend, now wife, at the time told me if I hated it, I should quit...so I did. This too by the way is a great way to live your life. If you hate your job, or whatever it is, stop doing what you hate and do something else. The hamster wheel is only a wheel if you stay on and keep moving nowhere. Otherwise, it's just a large object in an empty room which eventually turns to dust when not in use. You, in the body you have, only live once, so don't waste it being miserable. Seems too simple right?

As for the trades, my girlfriend had borrowed a miter saw from a friend and was going to replace all her own base trim. She was living in a house in Bowie, Maryland, and they had the old, small, rounded edge base trim. She was installing the slightly newer larger trim with the beaded edge. To remove it, it is a good idea to use a razor blade knife to score the caulk and paint edge many times before prying the trim loose from the wall. Make sure you utilize a scrap piece of trim, as a fulcrum point behind the bar and against a stud section, before you pry. This will prevent the pry bar from leaving an indentation in the wall. Also, I would recommend a small pry bar better suited for removing trim. Otherwise, you will have to repair wall damage from the gaps left by the bar (not a big deal if you know how, but major problem if not) … lessons learned. If, however, you are removing trim that was stained, you will most likely not be dealing with caulking, so you can skip past the scoring part.

I decided I was going to win her over by helping her and eventually taking over the project. I think I asked my father about how to cut the trim corners (this was before Youtube). You can set the angle of your saw to 45 degrees and cut both ends to the opposing angle. Or you just cut one side at that angle, and use a coping saw to cut out the thick part of the angle cut for a more precise connection. Once I was given this information, it came down to practice. After this encounter and a few days of physical work, I was hooked. Up until this point, I had believed the trades were an option for the lower class, as I had been convinced that if you wanted to be an achiever in life, you needed college. I went to college (Community then St.Mary's College of Maryland), but decided a life in the trades was the right path for me. That was the year I realized the immense value and understanding of the trades meant for me. Eventually I went from being a super senior (I was 24 senior year) in college to a business owner. I couldn't get enough of learning how to do things in the home. I went from learning how to cut and hang trim, to drywall finish and repair, to painting and house washing. I ended up settling on painting or specializing rather. I ended up earning an MHIC (Maryland contractor's license) and a Class C Virginia license.

One of my gym buddies at the time (while attending college) owned a painting company, and he taught me many things. However, I will never forget my first experience with him. My first day on the job, he handed me a brush (I recommend Purdy angled sash —they are the best), and I went to work cutting around a light. As professionals, we do not tape. I painted the shit out of that light, and almost got fired not long after starting the day. Luckily, he gave me another chance and showed me the right way to hold and manipulate the brush to cut correctly. Within a short while of working for him part time, I was painting entire houses without him needing to be there. When I realized he was driving nice new vehicles, and I could barely keep my old van operating, it was time to think bigger about my future. I went from getting paid thirteen dollars an hour, to typically charging fifty to sixty an hour under my ownership. Even in my mid-twenties, I believed in virtue and character and did not take side work for his customers —there were ample opportunities. Thankfully, I had the ability to see beyond the short term and wanted to stay on the right side of karma —this is before I understood the universe and interconnectivity of our species.

Eventually, because of my experience and confidence in the trades, I was able to move my family three and half hours south to be closer to my mother-in-law. Prior to moving from Maryland, we had earned our MHIC Contractors license (which was no small accomplishment at the time) and began generating business quite easily. This would be short lived, as within the next two years, we decided to relocate further south. Subsequently, we opened our painting business in fall of 2008 in Southern VA. Acquiring a license in Virginia was a much simpler process. I attended an eight-hour class, and then I was a licensed contractor.

The trades are also why I have never had any fear of making a living in my adult years. They are called the trades for a reason. I have a friend, who is also a firefighter, and he helped me out a little bit, painting years ago. He eventually went further with his knowledge seeking and began purchasing houses to repair and sell, and eventually rent. Because of his knowledge of the trades, he now owns six houses and does all the routine maintenance on his own. Another friend of mine supports his family with the trades and got his start by buying a home and flipping it. He did all the repair and rework himself, and now owns a busy remodeling company.

I have been able to barter for some really cool stuff via the trades. We painted the interior of a hot yoga studio in exchange for a few years of free memberships and massages; this is also a similar trade scenario we had with the Jiu-Jitsu studio that awarded me my brown and black belt. We also bartered painting for chiropractic service and landscaping work on our home.

You can also utilize trade knowledge to help out others, via a time and skill donation. I helped declutter a house and perform demolition for a remodel once, for a family in need. I also donated my time and skills working on the exterior of the museum (which was a nonprofit) in our hometown. We also utilized our business to sponsor many little league teams and community organizations.

When I returned to the fire service, the training center needed painting, so I spent a few days painting all the floor and door trim to help express my gratitude for the second chance at my fire career. As for charity organizations, Christmas in April would be a good example of this. Also, I painted a fence and some ceilings for a buddy in the fire department, because I had the time and wanted to do something nice. There have been a plethora of other moments, where I have donated my time, but too many to recount. My chief, who owns his own house wash business, has offered his time on many occasions washing homes for friends during times in need; what a great way to spread love and spread light in the world!

There is no limit to how far the trades can take you. If you are ever given the chance to work with a friend or family member and learn a trade, I highly recommend you take the opportunity to learn. Many of my close friends own their own trade companies. It's also one of the only recession proof and recently proven Virus proof career paths there is. Our calls for painting work actually increased during the Virus, but we were able to refer the leads to others who were still in the trades and needed the work.

When we moved in 2008, during the recession, many pre-established businesses were booming, and we did not find it difficult to get ours off the ground. We would be pumping gasoline and see no less than six different painting vans drive by over the course of a few minutes. Obviously, we were tuned into looking for these things, but it also proved that there was enough work for everyone. The world is abundant and there will always be enough work for everybody. There is no need to be overly competitive and think others are taking food from your table —this simply isn't true. Also, if you give in value and effort more than monetary compensation, you will not only make it, but you will make it big. Once our business took off, we could not keep up with all the work that was flowing to us.

The other great thing about the trades, is you won't go into debt while learning them, unlike anything that requires a college degree. Instead of amassing massive student loans with the hopes that your hard work will pay off when you land your dream job (and there is no guarantee you will land your dream job), you get paid while learning the job. I know all too many people who trusted the college route, only to become police officers or hot tub repair men, with years of debt ahead of them. I am not implying either of those are not cerebral or virtuous careers, but their degrees did not exactly correlate to their careers...and certainly were not needed. Take police or fire for example, often once you are in those careers, they will pay or reimburse you for college classes taken to enhance your career.

There is more tangible value than just working in the trades for a living, as all men should have a basic understanding of how to do basic drywall repair, painting, caulking etc. You want to impress a girl? Repaint her living room. We charge $400 for that, as we can paint (two coats/walls only) the typical living room in two and a half hours (this includes setup, moving furniture, painting and cleanup). Drywall work is even more lucrative. I recently gave a buddy a bid for some drywall work that I quoted for 600. I won the job, but realized our schedules did not line up, so I referred him to a different company. They quoted the work for 1,200. There is money to be made.

As for your lady, want to impress her even more? Soft wash her parents' house, recaulk their windows or hang crown moulding...offer something. I have worked many hours at my mother in law's home and my parents' house too. It not only feels good doing nice things for the ones you love, but it's also an amazing feeling when you put on a tool belt or bust out the painting tools —like it's in our DNA, like driving fast and listening to loud music in the younger years; you just feel like a man.

If you plan to have children, a good understanding of home repair will save many arguments and possibly disasters. When I was in class (it was a one-day class in VA) to receive my contractor's license, the instructor told us about divorce's that had occurred because of contractor failures during large home improvement projects. I had also witnessed firsthand how invasive contractors can be when they are in your home, oftentimes extending the time and cost expectation leading to tension and stress. We eventually avoided working with other contractors for this reason. It was nothing personal but trying to maintain a schedule around so many other tradesmen was nearly impossible —probably why most painters have been relegated to alcoholism. You think I am proliferating a stereotype? We fired one of our best employees because he was caught drinking on the job, and he had one of those breathalyzers in his vehicle. He was what has been dubbed a "functioning alcoholic". When we asked him how he would handle the situation if he was in our shoes, he said he would not fire himself. Tough situations call for tough decisions. I have repainted our house and repaired drywall many times because of my two Tasmanian devils, and our dogs. My father always modeled hard work when I was growing up, and even to this day. Last month during a visit to their house, my dad was telling me he was removing the old floor from his outdoor bar and cabana and replacing it with new composite decking. He injured his knee doing so; the man is 70 years old and still working on his stuff; that's impressive.

He also modeled the importance of playing an instrument (we are both drummers and that is manly) and having weights at home, as he still jams downstairs to the classics and picks up the weights weekly too. He just sent me a text about his tricep burn from a killer workout, real men never slow down.

The key is to learn some basics to just about everything. If you want to eventually make a great living, then specialize. But it's nice when you can perform basic maintenance on your own home and help out your friends for free beer and good conversation.

In my home, I have replaced storm doors, reglazed windows, repaired my washing machine, dryer, water heater, HVAC system, interior phone lines, and cabinets. I Installed the new dishwasher and garbage disposal. I have added crown molding, crown lighting, and removed outdated sections to my cabinets with updates added. I have repaired and replaced minor plumbing issues, fished wires through walls to hide the wires after hanging a flat screen television. I have replaced worn lights, interior and exterior, and replaced pipe vent flashing and worn electrical switches and receptacles. I have put in laminate flooring, refinished our hardwood. I built our deck and did all the backfill when we replaced our bulkhead. I installed hammock posts, underground drains from our downspouts, replaced worn plumbing fixtures and epoxied our countertops. I also did the electric, hung and finished the drywall, hung the trim and doors and painted our addition. I also installed the tile (heated floor tile) in our addition (it was a large walk-in closet with a walk-in shower, toilet room and master bath with two sinks). I have repainted the ceilings and walls multiple times in the past 12 years and added an extra room to our home via adding partition walls. My wife has helped with most of the above too.

I have been capable of all of this because I wanted to impress a girl all those years ago and have saved many thousands. I never would have known that I would get so much value out of the skills I have learned, but I do know it's one major reason I walk tall and feel like a man. This does not mean that you have to take up a trade to be a man, not at all. I have met many awesome men, who have no business holding a hammer, but they are also the reason tradesmen have work, and often large backlogs.

But a man who has no knowledge of the trades, and who pays a fair and honest wage for work rendered, that's a real man too. Fortunately, I did not deal with many bad customers with dubious motives. I have heard many horror stories about people not getting paid and having to take out mechanics liens to receive payment. This is up there with being a parsimonious tipper; people of this nature are the enemy of the trades and are also the type to go to contractor search sites with caustic and inflammatory reviews against small businesses. If the person you hired does the job right and satisfies the contract, pay your debt. I can't imagine the bad karma people attract when they treat hard working people this way. Don't misunderstand me, there are flawed or phoney professionals too.

One time we were painting the exterior of a home, for a repeat customer, and they had a roofing company installing a new roof. During the demo of the old roof, the workers were tossing the shingles off the second story roof. The shingles kept swiping the siding, and they were leaving unsightly dark marks on the light-colored vinyl siding. The workers were using Goof-Off to remove the marks; the only problem is Goof-Off melts vinyl, so it left an unattractive streak on the siding. My wife and I, being informed and good at our jobs, knew this about the product. The customer's neighbor caught them doing this and told the homeowner as did we, as the homeowner was a repeat customer, and we did not want to get blamed.

After you have been in the business a while, or been an adult long enough, you realize not everyone cares about being honest and culpable for their actions. The owner of the roofing company denied that they made the marks and tried to say it was us. Believe this, they even applied oil-based paint to the siding to make it look like it was us. Luckily, the paint we were using had a different consistency and color (and was water based), but this actually happened. In the end the roof leaked as well, and the roofer took no responsibility for their lousy work; he even had negative things to say about the homeowner.

All I can say is, the statement "you get what you pay for" holds true for the trades. On a quick side note, speaking of roofs. One of the easiest things to check with a small leak in the roof is the pipe vent boots that sit snug around the plumbing ventilation pipes. Near any and all of your plumbing you will have the vent pipes that extend from your roof. They help supply fresh air to help the water flow when leaving your home. Around all these pipes are flashing, usually with a rubber boot. I have seen hundreds of these fail over the years because over time, the rubber will become brittle, crack and fail. It's a quick fix to purchase a new boot and just slide it down the pipe. Keep this little nugget of information in mind next time you or a friend discovers a small leak. Luckily, we did everything in our power to keep our customers happy and had very little experiences in the way of dissatisfaction. We still get calls every week for work even though we are no longer operational.

I am a student of the game and vowed to try and imbibe every bit of knowledge I could about my trade. Also, for years I genuinely enjoyed my work, so enjoyed learning and expanding my knowledge base. My Knowledge of the trades has helped me immensely in the fire service. I understood things about building construction and building materials that gave me an instant advantage when checking homes for smoke scares and going to fires in residential settings. I was able to understand how most walls are 16 or 24 inches on-center, so if you need to breach a wall, you can guess somewhat accurately where to make your sheetrock knockouts. Understanding the thickness of certain kinds of plywood is important for roof ventilation purposes. I also understood why sometimes a switch or wall outlet would go bad and cause what we call smoke scares or just a faulty switch.

I have had many great conversations with other firefighters who understand the trades, and also helped newer and younger firefighters understand some of the tricks of the trade. The other great thing the trades have taught me is time management and business ownership, and no matter how far you go in your career, unless you are a foreman or CEO, you will never really experience the highs and lows of business ownership. When you are the owner of a small business, this means everything good or bad begins and ends with you. Because of this responsibility, we learned never to make excuses for our blunders and try to learn from every mistake.

This has carried me incredibly far in the fire service and life, where reputation and honesty are everything. Honesty and willingness to accept culpability are also great life traits. As you traverse your adult years, you will find that this has tragically become a rarity in our society. Next time you go outside, look around. You will probably see houses or large buildings, if you live in the city, just about everywhere. If you are in one of the last agrarian locations in the world, then you may see cows or goats or whatever, which just means you haven't had the aftereffects of gentrification yet. Notice how much construction, development and work has gone into your environment, and all the trades that were involved in the process. It's really amazing to take in and gratifying to know that even if the next age will be all digital, people will still need places to live, and companies will need places to store their product and robotronic creations. So why not secure your future by learning a trade.

If you are young or old (age really does not matter against the mind) and looking for the next possible career or just trying to add another line to your job experience list, try working a trade. You may discover that thing you were meant to do, or you may loathe the experience all together. Either way, you will be able to say you've had that experience. An advantage tradesmen will always have over everyone else is lack of desperation in their quest for long term employment. So many people feel stuck in their careers, and therefore slip into slow but definitive madness because they have accepted the illusion that options are limited.

The feeling of being stuck in a job is a terrible feeling, one that most people will endure in their lifetime. Placing all your eggs in one basket is the epitome of locking yourself into a position. Knowledge of the trades allows people an option to hit the reset button if their chosen career does not hold up to expectations. Think of the joy that would bring, knowing that you always hold the power to pick your future. Thankfully because of the trades, we all do.

# CHAPTER SIX: WOMEN

*"The true beauty in a woman is reflected in her soul."*

—AUDREY HEPBURN

*"Women are a labyrinth my friend."*

—CHIP DOUGLAS (CABLE GUY)

First off, don't get your hopes up gentlemen. Believe me, if I knew everything there was to know about women, I would rule the world, in its entirety. Unfortunately, I do not. However, I do know a few things about the opposite sex, and I will happily share some lessons learned. We shall begin with the world talk! Gentlemen, we do way too much talking, and this flaw doesn't always fade with age. I have spoken to my mother-in-law (she is a divorcee) about this, and she says men her age are just as bad at this skill as the younger generation, and she was in her 60s when she shared this with me. This was empirical evidence gathered from the many dates she endured after her divorce. I too have met many men in their later years that love to talk too much.

Confabulating with people should be a joyous experience with give and take. Women however are not that interested in what we have to say, at first. One great lesson I learned from a woman was to ask questions. Some people are really good at this skill, but most are not. Most of the public wants to talk about themselves and listen only long enough to interject their own thoughts or beliefs into a conversation. Don't believe me? Next time you go out with friends and meet someone new, pay attention to how much they inquire about you. Sure, they may ask a few perfunctory questions about how do you know so and so, or what is your name, but focus on whether they ask any real questions to find out anything about you. Even more prevalent is when you attend a gathering with friends or a small party, and there are people there you do not know. Oftentimes, the host will not even introduce you to them, and then the longer time goes without introduction the more awkward it becomes to approach each other.

You want to be a winning host, introduce people, and if you are not the host, go up to everyone, introduce yourself and ask them a few questions about themselves. But it is incredibly important the host makes the introductions. It's that simple, and once they have been introduced, get them talking. When we attended the "Breakaway Bourbon" night, my wife and I made sure to introduce people —spouses especially. That is why a small gym is so successful. I learn people's names and help reinforce it by constantly introducing new people. I have tried this experiment many times, and often when my wife and I are together. We know how this works, so we usually do the dirty work of asking questions and keeping the conversation flowing. I have attended many social gatherings, where guests may be strangers to each other, and the host introduces no one. It's madness.

If you do not have much planned in the way of going out, you can also try this experiment at work. Pay attention to how often your coworkers ask about you. I am not talking about the obligatory "how was your weekend" or "how are you today". I mean real conversation. You will be surprised to see how little people inquire about others. It doesn't make them bad people, and lord knows I do not like to spend much time with some people, as some people are energy vampires —again only wanting to talk about themselves and their problems. But even these interactions can sometimes be beneficial because they highlight all the positives that we all sometimes take for granted.

As far as talking to women, you have to overcome this malady and get the woman talking. Learn to be inquisitive. Ask them pointed and open-ended questions. Avoid questions that will traditionally yield yes or no answers. For example, avoid questions like "Do you like your job?" or "Do you watch sports?". If they say no or simply yes, it can oftentimes be a conversation killer. Instead ask how long have they been in their career field, and do they find the work enjoyable and gratifying and why? You could ask, do you follow any sports on television or dabble in any yourself, and if not, what do you enjoy doing in your free time? Now remember with all this advice, this is for adult women not the tweens of today. My fourteen-year-old studly mudly of a son does all that YOLO stuff on Snapchat. I know nothing about that stuff, and do not want to learn. But I will boldly make the assumption, once these younger folks age into adulthood, the skill of conversation will prove timeless and useful indeed.

Now, a very important concept to understand is confidence. The key is to command a presence of confidence and ease. Before you go out to begin your date, envision it going really well. Play the scenario in your head how you want it to occur in reality. The power of your thoughts is more incredible than any of us really know; read any book by Bob Proctor to experience this. Think positive thoughts and believe that you are a real man with lots to offer the opposite sex, and smile. Also, this goes without saying, but I will provide this advice anyway, shower and apply plenty of deodorant. Nothing says you do not care about making a good impression like being stinky and unclean. No amount of cologne can mask body odor, so don't even try it. As for everything else, once you get the woman talking, time starts to slip away, and before you know it, you both are having a good time.

Most men get hung up with looks. Don't get me wrong, you don't want to let yourself go and forgo showering and utilizing deodorant, but women are not as preoccupied with looks as we think they are. Sure, at first, looks are a good way to break the ice and snag their attention, but with enough practice of quality conversation, your looks will become less important and less noticeable to the ladies. So don't be hard on yourself. I on the other hand am a big fan of keeping my looks in check. My wife does the same. All too often, you see and talk to people that were in great shape when they got married, but then they allowed life to carry them away. They let themselves go. I have always felt it is my obligation to try and maintain and hold myself to a high standard, physically and mentally. I took my wife away from the dating world. The least I can do is maintain the physical aspect of the man she married while constantly trying to improve upon the mental.

Keep in mind, if you are two timing asshat that already understands the ladies and has cheated on your girlfriend or wife, then this chapter is not for you. Infact, change your ways or quit reading my stuff. I do not want to be associated with men who act in such ways. I write for the guys that think with their hearts and minds and not their phallus. Most often these are the types of fellas that are bashful and may need some help launching the conversation in the beginning. I too struggled a little bit in my younger adult years, but since have discovered the secret.

Often overlooked, is the gift of humor. Humor is huge with the ladies. Take it from me, I have been married for a long time, and still enjoy making my wife laugh. Do not try too hard with this, as it will happen organically if you allow it. Keep it simple in the beginning. Remember the open-ended questions, and as your lady friend begins to open up about herself, that is your opportunity to throw in some quips and giggles. My wife and I have lived together and worked together through two businesses. Most men I have talked to would say, "I could never work with my wife". Well, I have, and we are stronger for it. I can still make her laugh to this day, and she can do the same. So, I know this process works.

You can also employ the law of attraction in dating too. If you want a certain kind of woman, set your intentions of finding that kind of woman. Be confident and patient. The right one will be out there waiting, so don't think you have to settle. That is one of the biggest and most common reasons marriages fail. Like careers, people settle. If you are looking for a specific type of person in your life, think about it, believe in it, and go out and get it. There are over seven billion people on this planet, so the right person is out there. I repeat, you do not have to settle. In the beginning, don't rush the relationship. If you start the relationship with a void, because of settling, eventually you will become complacent which may lead to lack of care, or you will just go out eventually and get what you wanted in the first place with no regard for the person you settled for; this mode of thinking is selfish and wrong, but people do it every day. So, check all the boxes you can while dating. Don't ghost the ladies either, unless you are uninterested of course, but even then, finding a polite way to let them know you are uninterested is a good way to end it. At the end of the day, you are interacting with a human being, so be nice.

There is no set standard of time that you have to wait to call or text. Just don't do so in a nervous or worrisome fashion. The ladies will not like that vibe, and it emanates the opposite of confidence, desperation. Which is never sexy. Chivalry, as the saying goes, is not dead, and it never will be. Women cannot resist when a man does something nice and thoughtful. I feel like an absolute stud when I open the door for my wife or carry something heavy for her. Again, like the conversation bit, it shows you are thinking and care about them. Also, don't forget to compliment your lady on her nice dress or fresh, exciting hairdo, as women do appreciate when a man notices these things.

Women also do not want to become a part of your obsessions. They do not want to only sit around and watch you play video games, work on cars or watch movies in your living room. Women are not complete enigmas, and like most humans, enjoy variety. Assuming you have a job and some fun money, you could purchase tickets to a play, or make reservations to a fancy restaurant. You could go on a nature hike or nature walk with your lady. There are endless opportunities and ways you can surprise a lady with a thoughtful good time. Don't think that taking your lady home to play Call of Duty is her idea of a good time because it isn't...no matter how much she pretends it is. Now, if playing said game is on your must have list, then make sure your lady does love playing that game, as having things in common is an obvious suggestion. I urge you to comport yourself in this way, especially during the first six months of the relationship, but the real prize comes when you continue to do your best for your lady after the typical novelty period of the relationship.

During the beginning months, learn to cook. So, when you guys move in together, you can be the house chef and cook delightful meals. Is cooking manly? Oh, yea it is! It shows creativity, initiative and independence which when a woman is looking for a mate and possible father to her unborn children, are top list qualities. Plus, everybody eats, so learning to cook is valuable no matter how you spin it. Also, tossing aside a fast-food wrapper, because of being too lazy to cook, has and will never be sexy. I love pickles and ketchup, but when the car smells like it, it's time for an intervention. Just as important, do not be a doormat. All too often, I have seen my guy friends date a girl, do everything she says, only to get shit on because he was willing to do everything demanded of him; typically, it's with another guy that just wants to get physical with their girl and is willing to say no to her demands.

I have also witnessed this with one of my married friends. Prior to his marriage, we went out shopping for our ladies, and I bought something cheap and useful for my wife. He however stated he had to purchase something expensive and extremely thoughtful to surprise her, as his girl would be upset and disappointed if he did not. Not one year after being married to her, she cheated on him with another man that she worked with. I am not saying be thoughtless and devoid of creativity with your relationship, but display a backbone and do not allow ultimatums into your relationship, especially when it comes to something like gift giving.

My wife has never told me if I don't buy her this or that, or do this or that, she would be mad, or our relationship would suffer. If she did, I would communicate to her that said behaviour would not work and to cut it out. I'd also probably half-jokingly threaten to give her a spanking for this transgression...the problem there is she'd probably enjoy it. Like I said, I've been in the marriage world for 15 years, and I did not settle; therefore, it's still adventurous and fun. Fuck all the television shows that say otherwise. I got news for you. If you are sitting around tainting your soul with that garbage, you don't really have a clue, and those assholes are being paid to convince you of their message.

You see that is the other secret, be a man. Do not allow the media and television to raise and inspire you. All the TV anchors I have seen lately are all fabulous without a scratch on them or any dirt under their shoes or fingernails —they are not real. They probably could not change a flat tire. They are fictitious facsimiles of what real men should be, adorned in makeup and reading from a script. Regarding television, on one end you have the real-life screw up (that declared he was HIV positive, after being diagnosed four years earlier) as the so-called alpha male lead-role example, and on the other just about every man in every commercial you see nowadays...you know the meek, skinny or rotund, shy patsy type. Even the lead character of the show *Home Improvement* was the butt of the joke; I know my references (I do not waste my time anymore getting lost in false reality aka watching television) are outdated, but they still hold water and show how long and pervasive the message has been in existence. Do not emulate either of those stereotypes, as there is a reason that is being portrayed as the new man, because people fear the alpha male.

But a true alpha male is not toxic, and the ladies cannot resist being seen with and chasing the alpha. Also, alphas don't run around calling themselves alphas, as they know they are alphas. So, if you think you are an alpha and claim to be, I'm almost certain there is a quiet, mild mannered dude in your group that has your number. I have witnessed there are more wanna be alphas than true alphas. You will know the difference by which one talks with their actions and which one with their mouth. Most real men do not brag about their skills or accomplishments or put others down or below them. Instead, the real ones are true to themselves, and this is the alpha that the ladies cannot resist.

Affection is also important to ladies, and should be to men too, as this is how you get your souls to mesh and share energies. Don't be afraid to lay a smooch on your lady or smack her on the behind every once in a while. This also helps to keep the relationship fresh and fun, as it is up to you to keep things from going stale. Once you have entered into the kind of relationship that allows for this type of affection, life can seem like heaven around you, and this my friends is the prize that only a good life can grant you. Happy hunting fellas.

# CHAPTER SEVEN: FATHERHOOD

*"Every father should remember one day his son will
follow his example, not his advice."*

—CHARLES KETTERING

I grew up in the 80s, which was basically the school of hard knocks compared to today's softer times. The only thing people were allergic to back then was boredom, and you could still hear children playing outdoors year-round. Every day was a testimony to the usefulness and necessity of tetanus shots and peroxide. Most likely, my mother bought peroxide by the case, when my brother and I were young. I have heard so many adults refer to the current pediatric age group as the snowflake generation, but my two sons are not snowflakes, and I know other true men with sons who are also real males.

For example, a firefighter friend broke his finger on the job and required a month off from work. You may ask, well what is wrong with that? By comparison however, my fourteen-year-old dislocated his, it was at a 90 degree angle from the knuckle, from catching a low fast thrown football at football camp. The only thing that saved his finger from breaking through the skin (the angle of dislocation was severe) was that he was wearing thick leather football gloves. They forced it back in place (in the ER), and he was back to catching footballs, and lifting weights in under a week.

Not to be outdone by the machismo of his older brother, my youngest son has a reputation to not be trifled with. A much older child picked on him a few years back, and my son pulled the Ralphie bully beatdown from Christmas Story; only, my son had better technique because of wrestling and jiu-jitsu, and I think you could actually understand the profanity streaming from his foam adorned mouth. There is a good chance most people would be terrified of this situation, but when I heard from the flabbergasted parent that my "sweet young man" went on a rampage to defend himself, I found that two young men were able to settle their differences with a bit of fistacuffs to be acceptable. Imagine if the leaders of our great country settled things this way...we most likely would not have a frail 78-year-old apparition that struggles to climb stairs or remember what his own name is, as the president of the most powerful country on earth. For perspective, my mother-in-law who has arthritic knees from previous knee surgeries, and is in her 70s, climbed the Luray Cavern steps with relative ease, and there was not one fancy camera there to photograph the moment.

So, the saying, "they don't make them like they used to" is false because mine were made tough. Why is this? Well, the first thing, I did not push my sons to be great or peak in their younger years —yes, I said younger years. In elementary and early middle school, so many dads were living vicariously through their sons, and making their sons' lives miserable because of it. You think stage moms are intense, so are sports dads. You saw all these amazing young athletes that were forced to be perfect and win. It was all about winning. I cared not about winning, because I was still and am still living and learning and understood the value of going out and learning while having fun. I care about learning and the experience, and this is what I encourage for my sons. Also, I know so many men my age that are now broken from years of abuse and countless injuries from the physical traumas they endured playing youth sports. Those years are miles on the body, and they add up.

I remember having a conversation with one of the head coaches whose son was around nine or ten. His son was the star running back, and the coach (his father) was incredibly hard on him. The coach told me that his father had pushed him so hard in his youth to wrestle that he quit in high school. I found it ironic that he was doing the same thing to his son but did not either realize it or care. I did not feel like it was my role to force my son to be the best. If he signed up for something, I would not let him quit until the season's end, but I did not helicopter parent and expect perfection. My expectation was for them to learn, improve and enjoy the experience. Because over time, if I exert an extreme level of pressure upon my sons, they would grow to resent me for it, and possibly resent the sport or activity as well.

Here we are five years later, and my oldest son is one of the biggest, strongest, and most motivated kids out there. He doesn't limp off the field after every play like some of his teammates who already have loads of miles on their body. Last month, he was one of the youngest attendees at a football camp, yet in the top five percent in tallest and musculature. He will be partaking in another football camp tomorrow, as the Virus still has a moratorium on school sports. Luckily, camps are still an option. During the editing phase of this chapter, my son (being a freshman) was a starter for his JV season and was a second string for the varsity postseason; not bad for a kid who has not played since elementary school.

The other interesting dilemma I have seen so many fathers generate is they repeat the same habits that they did not enjoy from their youth. For instance, I was talking with a buddy and he said it used to drive him nuts when his dad would work in the garage and not say anything to him about it. His father would then come in the house angry because he never went out to help his father with whatever he was doing. My friend then proceeded to tell me that he was out working in the yard and his young teen did not come out to offer help. He said this upset him, so he lectured his son about it. This is absolute madness, but I see it all the time. If you do not like something about how you were raised, you do not have to repeat it; you have the power to interact differently.

My father used to pull this stunt too, and I never understood, even as a child, why he wouldn't just ask me to assist or help. If I want or need help, I ask my sons for help. I do not assume they will come outside and offer, as I am a realist, and know they would rather not move from the couch. But they are always willing when I need them.

Playing mind games with your children rarely yields the results you hope they will; resentment and misunderstanding are typically the end result of such habits. Just communicate. I have witnessed modeling this lack of communication rarely yields the results intended, and often this is the same way interactions are dealt with by other adults —again, this process often leads to tension, and it does not teach your child anything about direct communication. No matter how bad you want it, your family members will never develop clairvoyant powers. Your assumptions and desires are only met when you let people know they exist. If you predict you will need help with whatever project you have planned, prime your children by letting them know ahead of time. Because I approach projects this way, I know I have raised them to be helpful and willing when their help is needed. If you set the precedent that whining or complaining when help is needed is not acceptable, then they are typically happy to help in small doses.

Another thing my wife and I chose to do differently was not treat our children like second class citizens. I recall all too often growing up and hearing, "hit the bricks" or "go peddle your papers" ...basically code for getting lost kids. We were told we should be seen and not heard. Needless to say, it was a struggle learning to communicate in my early adult years because I did not have much up close modeling or practice.

I am not complaining, as *Tony Robbins* says in the documentary, *I am not your Guru* you have to thank them (my parents) for the bad things, or what we perceive as negative too; so I am grateful for all the moments I enjoyed and did not enjoy about my youth, and understand the importance of taking the good and forgiving everything else. But again, I modeled my communication goals on doing things differently, and I allowed my sons to have a voice and communicate. The balance act of this privilege did sometimes cause confusion, as my fourteen-year-old that is now my size or slightly taller, has had to be reminded that I am the boss even though I allow him to have a voice and opinion in the day-to-day happenings. But his confidence is appreciated.

The most important life skill I have tried to teach my boys is honesty, well kindness too, but honesty is number one. We do not punish our boys as harshly if they are honest. Because of this, my sons (my oldest especially) are supremely honest. He has told my wife some disturbing (not criminal) things, but he is a teenager and has done nothing worse than I did when I was his age. But I have met my share of dirtbags that cannot keep track of all their lies, and I am proud to be raising the opposite of this. The be kind, be humble, be ready mindset is exactly how I raised my boys, even before I realized this was the summation of our message at the studio. We realized early on that if our boys were to make it and thrive in this world, we wanted them to understand the power of love, empathy and honesty. But also, we wanted them to be the living, walking example that overt kindness is never weakness. Basically, they learned to kick ass and defend themselves in case the situation was ever warranted. Someday they may need to exert themselves physically, and they will be ready.

Enrolling your youth in martial arts is a great way to ensure they will be ready if they must defend themselves. We would all love to believe they will never need to defend themselves, but deep down I believe we all know this to be false. According to the website, *Rainn.org* their article *Campus Sexual Violence Statistics,* shows that 26.4% of undergraduate females and 6.8% of males experience some form of sexual violence on campus. Luckily, more women and young ladies have been flocking to the jiu-jitsu mats to hopefully generate some violence prevention power. Interestingly, because of mirror neurons, young men having positive role models and learning kindness, are less likely to grow and become sexual deviants. Also, I have read that a sociopathic personality is a learned behavior, so the onus is on us, as parents, to display kindness and love. The best way to ensure our children grow up to be kind adults is to teach them kindness and weaponize them with the knowledge to defend themselves, and possibly others. Also, martial arts may become the activity or sport that they enjoy and decide to dedicate their time and heart to.

The most important facet of being a dad, I have come to realize, is you are someone your son or daughter looks up to. Recently, my son and I had a small falling out that lasted about an hour. The event culminated with me taking his phone and video games and requiring him to communicate with me. Once his anger settled, he was able to tell me more clearly why he was so upset. It boiled down to the fact that I was not spending enough time with him, and when I did talk to him, it was usually to correct an unfavorable behavior. Basically, I was acting like a version of a father that would irritate and bother me. The next day, I drove him to his football camp, and spent a few hours with him. During the conversation, he said I was one of two males he knew that he looked up to. I never assume I am an important person in people's lives, so this was something I was meant to hear, and it warmed me deeply to the core.

I understood by his reaction the night before, something had to change, and it needed to change from the top...from me. Had I been too proud and stubborn to accept I needed to be the harbinger of said change, my son would have most likely played along to act the part but would develop subsurface resentment that would have caused an inevitable drift in our relationship.

Remember, even in our relationships with our loved ones, moments of tension or discomfort are there to remind us something needs to change, or we should be doing something better. That is the most crucial time to make forward progress in any relationship. Our actions and reactions will never lead us to failure if we never quit and continue to strive towards growth and understanding.

Coincidentally, when I made my return to the larger fire department, I had to endure a psychoanalysis assessment. The focus of the psychologist's questioning was my relationship and feelings about my father. I had been a couple years into my self-growth endeavors and 38 years old, so I understood the strategy he was playing, or rather understood what he was trying to decipher with his questions; but then I also realized the importance of a fruitful father son relationship. Luckily, I have allowed my sons a voice and opinion and continue to strive to keep a good relationship with them. Also, I have encouraged them to be unapologetically male.

There has been an ongoing onslaught of late against manhood and manliness in general. There are entire groups of people who have made it their goal or agenda to find fault with the message of being male. Some people with or without vaginas have made it their mission to hate humans who were born with penises. Hate is hate, no matter how smooth or well delivered the message. If we raise our sons to be kind, honest, loving, competent but also capable of ass-kicking young men, all the noise and chaos will seem like flies or inclement weather at worst, to our sons...nothing more than a nuisance — and with the ability to circumnavigate attempts to usurp the ship, true power exists for our future and theirs. Go forth young men and conquer the world on your terms; let's empower and enrich our sons with knowledge and love, so they may do so with aplomb and kindness in their hearts.

# CHAPTER EIGHT: MARRIAGE

*"No matter what happens to us, everyday spent
with you is the best day of my life."*

—NOAH (FROM THE NOTEBOOK)

*"Fortunate indeed is the man who selects a wife whose
influence on him is inspiring and constructive."*

—ANDREW CARNEGIE

I never went to school so that I could label myself an "expert" on marriage, and if I had, I would still know nothing of what I know today from actual experience and love. I find it peculiar and strange that people can attend classes to learn how to give advice to married couples, and yet find it more peculiar that couples will listen to said expert. We have married friends who seek advice and council from divorced "experts" —say what? But my incredulous behavior comes from a guy that was able to figure out the secret to sustaining a good marriage, without the help of a love doctor or a single marriage counselling session —though I am not discrediting any of those options. Aside from watching a Dr. Phil episode or two with my wife (followed by Super Nanny) during the early years, our experience and advancements have come from within.

Interestingly, I was watching a video to earn continuing education credits for my Paramedic cert, and I found out my wife and I were already doing what studies have proven to be effective via the magic relationship ratio discovered to be true by Dr. Gotman and Levinson. They claim this is a ratio of five to one: For every negative interaction, you need five positive ones to maintain a strong and healthy marriage. I absolutely agree with this ratio, as we had discovered this through trial and error, and it has proven necessary for a thriving marriage.

> *"A wife of noble character is her husband's crown, but a disgraceful wife is like decay in his bones."*

> **PROVERBS 12:4**

I suppose I am one of the lucky few, as I did witness a good marriage that still lasts today, growing up. And I am currently in a thriving marriage. On the other side of the spectrum, I have had friends who have been divorced multiple times, and not quite understand why they were a part of the divorce loop. One of these friends eventually thanked my wife and I for giving them advice and have since gone on to find happiness in their current marriage. Never would I consider myself an expert, but if Google states that fifty percent of marriages end in divorce, and successive divorce averages are even higher, then perhaps I know more about what every other person does regarding keeping a marriage intact.

From what I have witnessed, I do believe you can marry the wrong person. I do not think marrying for looks "only" is ever the right reason, but I also believe the physical connection and satisfaction is important, especially in the beginning years. I remember I had a buddy tell me, just before he got married, that his wife would not provide certain things during their intimate moments. She told him certain favors felt like a derogatory expression towards women. I do not think it is manly or a good idea to share your bedroom routine with friends; however, this person told me this in a way that proved he didn't necessarily agree with her stance on the matter and was looking for sympathy from a friend. The good thing was she was willing to tell him what she was and was not willing to do before entering the marriage, which then gave him a chance to accept or deny these parameters. These feelings do not make people grotesque or vulgar, and I think it is important both partners understand the wants and needs of each other, prior to engaging in a lifelong commitment. This serves as an example of why some marriages fail.

*"It is not a lack of love, but a lack of friendship*
*that makes unhappy marriages."*

—FRIEDRICH NIETZSCHE

Like a conversation about children, many believe with enough time they can convince their spouse or partner to change their minds about whatever, and oftentimes huge and important ones. In the beginning, my wife told me she wanted children. At the time, we were dating, and she was already employed and making great money working a government job. So, the idea was not extreme financially, but it took me a little time to warm up to the idea because of the level of responsibility. Not to say she was not worth having children with, but I was not sure I was a fitting person to lead the role. After having a second chance at dating my wife (the first time we did not go on more than a few dates) I decided, or rather my inner being woke me up to the truth, she was my soulmate, and I would gladly have children with her. Interestingly, she was told by her doctor that it would be difficult for her to conceive, so we should get right to it. She was around 29 at the time. Rendering her pregnant took no time at all, and before I had time to put a ring on her finger, she was pregnant; I had just turned 25, and it was good.

I did not have money or much in the way of established credit at the time, so I purchased a spurious diamond for my wife. She did not demand a large diamond, or an authentic diamond, or an expensive wedding; she just wanted me. Because of my experience, I would say a woman who demands a lavish rock to be a red flag, but so many men have bought into the idea that if we do not procure an expensive diamond, then we must stall the marriage.

We ended up marrying through the justice of the peace, and subsequently having our dinner ceremony at a local restaurant on a Wednesday. I remember a lady at the bar asked, "who gets married on a Wednesday?" I returned fire with "who drinks alone on a Wednesday?". I do not tell you this to encourage you to marry this way, but only to prove you do not need to convince yourselves or anyone else with elaborate and expensive displays of overt opulence, that your marriage is real. I have been to many elaborate and fantastic weddings encased in opulence and beauty, and could absolutely afford one today, but would never believe they are more likely to survive because of it. Ultimately, It comes down to love and feeling. If you are lacking on the inside, no amount of glamour and razzle dazzle will make a difference. I see all too often on online forums, where guys are talking about settling because they do not want to be alone, or they feel they will not be able to find someone they will get along better with. Any time I have settled for anything you know what has subsequently occurred, buyer's remorse.

With marriage, you are buying into an idea, an idea that could lead to everlasting enjoyment, or what feels like a prison sentence. I did not settle when I married my wife, and prior to me, my wife had just about assumed she would not find a fitting partner because she decided not to settle with her previous relationships. But, because we were both willing to hold out for what we were really looking for, we found each other. Fifteen years into our marriage, a common component of our marriage is hanky-panky. We also show our love in public, nothing inappropriate, but the typical sophomoric stuff, a smooch here and a butt slap there...and in front of our sons. Again, not intentionally, but the little freeloaders are omnipresent. My wife has commented before that her parents never showed affection in front of her and her siblings growing up; ironically, her parents also ended their marriage in divorce.

A girl I dated once showed me a family video of her parents, and her and her siblings asked her father who the prettiest girl was. He said "Stevie" (as in Stevie Nicks). In the video, her and her brothers all said, "but what about mom?" And he looked at the camera without a change in his tone and repeated "Stevie". I thought this was disrespectful at the time, and still maintain that belief. Her parents were divorced. Years prior, when I was around ten years old, I remember watching the movie The Last Dragon. There was a scene in that movie with an attractive singer, and I recall asking my father if he thought she was as gorgeous as I did. My dad however responded by saying my mother was the hottest woman he had ever seen; my mother was in ear-shot. To my chagrin, he didn't falter in his opinion. Regarding the woman in the movie, he could care less, or that was the example he set for me.

My folks are still married. You see, I now realize that even if my dad thought she was the most gorgeous woman in existence, he married my mother, and real men do not say things to hurt the ones they love, especially not a woman. They do the opposite and go out of their way to make the ones they love feel appreciated and cared about. Chances are though, he did feel that my mother was that beautiful, as an amazing marriage has a way of doing that to you. As for the example of my ex-girlfriend's father, I thought that was disrespectful to say in front of his wife, and it would stay in the layers of my memory that shape me as the husband I am today. If my boys were to ever ask me who I thought was beautiful, the words "your mother" would shoot from my mouth like a rocket. I never heard my father speak ill of his marriage or my mother, and my boys will never hear a negative or derogatory statement about their mother from me.

As far as my eyes could see, my parents were a team, and oftentimes against my brother and I...as it should be. Another time I was painting a neighbor's house, and they had teenage children. The neighbors were probably in their late 30s or early 40s. I had only been married for a year or so at the time. As I was painting their living room, the wife got to talking about her marriage. She said it was not like the movies, in a monotone voice. I remember thinking that is sad, as a marriage should be like the movies; marriage probably should not emulate a movie like Eyes Wide Shut, as that movie is very strange, and feels like a porno, but certainly like the Notebook; that one made me shed a few tears too, which is still manly. I have never lost the gusto for my marriage, and I think that is the key. Don't treat it like one of your material objects, or like Mitch Hedberg's joke about pancakes, "all exciting at first, but by the end you are sick of them." You must keep it fresh and exciting. If there are things you are into, like stockings and heels, ask your wife to wear those things. You also must make time for each other in the bedroom. If you have little kids, attempt to set up times with a babysitter, so that you can have a few hours of alone time. I recommend making nice and becoming friends with your in-laws, as they proved to be invaluable during our boys' early years.

Another common theme, when talking to divorced friends was, they were never, or were rarely intimate with their spouse. One of my friends could not remember the last time he had shared intimacy with his wife. This is unnatural. God gave us marriage and intimacy for a reason. We need it, especially us men. If I were not receiving enough intimacy, I would communicate this to my wife. If she then refused, then I would be well within my rights as a man and husband to look for and find what I needed, w/in the confines of legal action of course. Instead of doing it this way, most people choose resentment and anger because of lack of communication, which then often leads to going outside the marriage to satisfy your needs and wants. Communication is not always the easiest or most comfortable option at first, but with practice you realize it's the only true way to move forward in your marriage.

Be honest. Lying is the quickest way to tank a marriage. We have even raised our boys to be honest. If they get in trouble, but are honest, the punishment is less severe. Life and reality should be this way. Think of all the changes that could be made in our society if people would choose to live honestly. Would lawyers be necessary? Not as often that is for sure. Our prisons would also have more vacant cells if honesty were encouraged in our society. Social media, cell phones and emails are things that married couples should be willing to share.

My wife and I share a Facebook page, Snapchat, and Instagram page. Neither one of us uses Twitter or any of the other many options available. We know the passwords to all our emails, and we are permitted to look at each other's phones any time we want to. Even with a shared account, I have had female colleagues send a wave to the FB account, only to be intercepted by my wife. If we did not share accounts, this would have to be something I would show my wife anyway, as nothing good would come from FB messaging with other women.

We also do not hang out all the time with other couples. All too often I see other couples who are out getting drunk together, and spending what little time they have together, with other couples. Then before you know it, they are swapping partners. This atrocious behavior happens more than people think, and it's disappointing —especially in the fire service. This is not to say that you should never party with friends, but I have known couples that only find joy when they are around their friends while imbibing alcohol, and this is a problem for intimacy. As far as the mention of possible infidelity, I can count on many fingers the number of couples I know this has happened to. There is no guarantee this will happen, but the happiest, most solidified couples I have known spend most of their time together, and typically sober. Platonic friends are also a problem. The comedian, *Chris Rock* offers an interesting and honest perspective on platonic friends; I suggest you give it a listen.

I realize we are living in modern times and all, but my wife and I decided early on to remove any non-same sex friends from our lives...meaning I do not hang out with other women alone and neither does she. It has never been a problem and losing those friends did not create a void in our lives. We also made this pact around 2004, many years before we had any social media accounts, but we still never hang out with members of the opposite sex to this day. I am not talking about being friendly with coworkers or students at our jiu-jitsu school. But she does not hang out with other guys, and I do not hang out with other girls. We have never regretted this decision. If you cannot make this happen, I urge you to look in the mirror and question the strength of your self-esteem and ego. If, however, you both decide to have an "open relationship", well then that is fair game for the both of you.

Another big issue is most people sweat the small stuff. As the saying goes, don't sweat the small stuff, which I think also lends itself to the concept of what you think about only grows. If you focus on the negative, you will see and find lots of negatives. A friend, who had been married four times, would tell me how he would get upset with his wife for leaving food out on the counter, or not cleaning the bathroom well enough or forgetting to pick up her underwear in the closet. I told him if it was a problem, where she did this every day, then he should politely communicate his frustration with her. But, if it happens occasionally, maybe he could just put the mayonnaise back in the fridge for his wife. I wondered maybe she was dealing with something stressful in her life that caused her to forget the little things.

My wife will forget and have little moments like these, but so do I. I am probably the worst, but we do not dwell on the small stuff. When it is time to clean the house, we team up and clean it together. It gets done faster, and we did something together.

Men do not realize this but cleaning the house and helping with house chores is very manly, and somewhat of an aphrodisiac. Plus, us men think we must flash a bunch of cash or take our shirts off while wiggling our hips is the way to exude sexiness. We are mistaken. A good woman (notice I said good) will find you sexy when you vacuum the house or display love for your children. Keep it simple fellas.

Something else my father never did was talk about my mother in any way but endearing. I too have never spoken ill of my wife, as she does not deserve that, and I could not think of anything negative to say if I tried. All too often I hear men speaking negatively about their wives to other people. This is not conducive to a good marriage. Do not do this, as this will only build momentum and eventually cause a collapse in your thinking and your marriage.

Sometimes we need to be reminded about all the great things in our lives, our wives included. When my wife and I were painting together, and I was tired most days from lack of sleep on the medic or fire engine, I was often grumpy and sometimes discourteous to my wife. My wife took it like a champ, but eventually communicated that it was not fun anymore, and something needed to change. One, we have always put our marriage before our careers. When I joined the fire service, we both agreed if it brought strain and hardship to our marriage, I would quit. Two, this was before I understood the secret. Once I changed my thinking, I realized it was not that my wife was slower than me or slightly less capable than me at painting, as she should be because I started about eight years before her and learning to paint was never one of her goals. It was that she was willing to reside in the tradesman trenches with me, get dirty and do what was necessary to run our business. I literally know only one other woman who has the gumption and work ethic of this woman, my mother.

Just about every weekend, when I was growing up, my parents would work on their house together. My mother would don her white-collar outfits (she worked a high stress government career) for work during the week and remain busy, in her physical labor clothes on the weekends. Regarding my wife's work ethic, an incredible epiphany occurred when we were on our hands and knees, staining a large deck together. It was Mother's Day, and she was outside in the sun working hard to earn money for our family beside me. I realized that day, she was the hardest working woman I knew. Most women will not even walk out to the mailbox on Mother's Day, or leave the couch, but my wife was slinging stain and working manual labor because our gym was shut down during the Virus. Instead of allowing Satan to rule my thoughts, and thinking about the negatives, I began to think about the positives and display gratitude. I made a list of all the things I was grateful for, every day, about my wife. Before long, I had a paradigm shift, and I no longer needed the list. I just felt gratitude for my wife like I never had. Since this happened, I have never again taken my wife and her immense work ethic for granted.

I was recently discussing gratitude in marriage with a married friend. He is younger than me and has been married a few years. He said he and his wife had been having some problems. So, I asked if he could make a list of ten things he is grateful for, regarding his wife. He seemed perplexed, so I asked could you think of five things? He still struggled. This is where it begins. Do not let your thoughts carry you so far away from your emotions of love and gratitude that it becomes impossible to see all the good things in your marriage. I quickly fired off ten things I was grateful for about my wife, and I meant them. If you are at this point in your marriage and want to keep it together but cannot rapidly find the things to be grateful for, this just proves a paradigm shift is needed; improvement is never a hopeless endeavor.

Spend the time thinking of everything your spouse does for you, or your kids or the household. Think of all the things to be grateful for and make this your daily habit to find and focus on the positives. If none of the above are a part of your reality, talk with your spouse and inform them of what you would like to have or experience in your marriage. Sometimes, the good things just happen, but most of the time it's the quiet conversations that generate your marriage wish list. Over time, it will become easier, and things will start to get better, if you are willing to put in the time to manifest this. If despite your best efforts, you are with someone you loathe and cannot generate a gratitude list, stop wasting both of your time, and end the marriage.

I have heard divorcees often say if only their spouse had come forward with their opinions on ending the marriage sooner, they could have saved valuable time, or they could have both received counseling to help curtail whatever problems they were having. Fear and habit takeover for most people, and they choose to stay in relationships that they despise, because the thought of being alone or starting over is frightening. But if it will inevitably end in separation, and you feel this to be true, why delay the inevitable. I have never been through a divorce, but I know many people that have, and I am an amazing listener. I have gleaned loads of information from the many that were willing to share their stories and memories. I am not advocating to quit your marriage, but if no matter how hard you try —maybe you have already tried counseling to no success—, you are miserable, disconnected, and despondent about the person you married, you probably married the wrong person. But not wanting to walk away out of fear or loneliness is selfish. What an awful existence, especially for the woman you married and promised to love and cherish. If I made my wife miserable and caused her constant stress instead of warmth and joy, I would hope she would have the courage to communicate this to me, and if that did not cause improvement, I would encourage her to leave me. But I will never treat her this way. Or honestly, I will never treat her this way again.

Not that long ago, prior to learning of the law of attraction, and understanding how to look for the positives and exude gratitude, I was quite moody on days we had to paint. I was still part of the sleeping society that drank the Kool aid and bought the lies that life was difficult, and you had to sprinkle a little misery in your everyday life to prove you were working hard enough to progress forward. Like most people, I was content to drift through life instead of stopping to think and make things better. My wife was on the painting job with me and often I was working with only a couple hours of sleep, as I was at one the busiest fire stations in the department. My wife had the courage to communicate to me that my attitude and daily discontent was beginning to make her life on the job unbearable.

My ego was bruised a little bit at first, but with much thought, I realized she was right. My realization of this culminated when I had an epiphany on the job —as aforementioned, she was working on Mother's Day, and I realized how completely and utterly delinquent my thinking had been, and my paradigm shift occurred like a building collapse in my heart and mind. Luckily, I had done enough good to outweigh the difficult times, but I have since made it my mission to appreciate the endless good that my wife provides for me, my sons and this universe, and my appreciation goes deeper than that.

I know many people who believe their adult years have earned them the right to remain steadfast and stringent in their beliefs and thinking. Unfortunately, these are the same people that have been conditioned to believe they have to look out for number one. I could have taken that gamble and told my wife to take a hike and decided to continue to treat her how I had been. Instead, I realized my best bud and life partner was asking for help, and I was the one with the steering wheel for change. I think about this all the time. I took my wife from the dating pool and promised her a good life. What kind of miscreant would I be if I did not deliver on this promise? She also promised to love me and do right by me, and she has not failed in this endeavor one bit.

Look, I make no guarantees you will find paradise in your marriage, but I believe this chapter to be a great roadmap to making it so. Be good and honest with those who you have chosen to love, and your marriage will be full of wonder and excitement. If you do not like something about yourself or your marriage, change it. Nothing is set in stone until you believe it is, and even the stone can be thrown into the abyss with intentions of starting over. Hubris and ego have no place in marriage. If you think you are setting a good example and being an alpha by remaining steadfast when you should be pliable, you are wasting valuable time stifling your relationship instead of growing it. The choice is yours. Most big decisions and changes are won by micro-decisions. Do not make the mistake and believe that a morning smile or a kiss on the cheek, whenever your wife enters the room, is wasted affection. Small actions yield big results, and small moments of affection are no different. Cheers to you and your relationship, and I hope time brings you immense joy and contentment.

# CHAPTER NINE: LEADERSHIP

*"Leaders are Readers."*

**—JIM KWIK (LIMITLESS)**

Congratulations, if you are still here imbibing wisdom, chances are you have what it takes to be a leader. But seriously, leadership...what a great concept. Leadership is an unspoken agreement that one person will help lead another, or many, with the hopes that when anything unpleasant happens, those that are supposed to be leaders will do the right thing and rise to the occasion. Like every chapter in this book, I have seen some great examples of both erudite and not so great leadership. Let us first example some not so stellar leadership qualities.

Early on in my fire career, we responded to a call for chest pain and breathing difficulty. Typically, an engine and a medic will respond for calls like this because this is deemed a serious call, and often much help will be needed. On this call, the patient was what is called a "frequent flier" in the industry; basically, they call 911 all the time for emergencies and non-emergencies... unfortunately mostly non emergencies. We have had people, who we know by name, who call so much they will step in the medic and hook themselves up to the monitor and proceed to check their own vital signs; this is not normal, but at three am in the morning, for the third shift in a row, your patience and sympathy are just about depleted —plus, they hook themselves up correctly and safely.

During this call however, an officer on scene took over the call and began displaying irate behavior with the patient. Because this officer was also a paramedic, no one told him to back down so they could run the call. I was still a probie at the time, or I would have stepped up to prohibit the officer from usurping our call —I have had to do so recently with a different officer...it happens.

The patient ended up receiving substandard care, and this time his reason for calling was legitimate. After the call, I had enough common sense to know that the call had gone off the rails because the officer took over when he did not need to, and he had lost his composure. This was the cliche in real time of too many cooks in the kitchen. Typically, on all EMS calls, the medics are responsible for running their calls unless an EMS captain is on scene. The officer on the aforementioned scene told me that it was okay, it could have happened to anyone, and not to feel too bad —as if to say it was my fault our call was a mess, if not a failure. I vowed that day to never do this when I am an officer. It seems we do live in a "pass it off" society, where it is becoming rare to see people accept responsibility for their blunders. Had the officer taken credit for his gaffe by overstepping the unspoken boundaries, when he did not need to —as well as losing his rapport with the patient —, I would have maintained nothing but respect for the guy.

Being a good leader is knowing when it is not your place to interject or run things, and when to allow your subordinates to maintain their own autonomy. If you ever want your group to grow, you must trust your staff to do their jobs, and if you do not trust your people, then there is a void in your training or preparation. It is no different than an owner of a company giving their trust to the foreman to run and manage things. Plans fall apart when this type of interaction is not allowed to occur. When people from one level of the hierarchy unnecessarily disrupt lower levels, things begin to fall apart. More importantly, blaming others instead of accepting responsibility is cowardly, and not at all conducive to leadership.

Accepting fault when it's due is the quickest way to take power back and earn respect. So many people would rather play the blame game and remain victims to circumstance than to accept their faults and move on. I have had countless moments where I had made a mistake and immediately owned up to it. I swear so much stuff happens, it's as if I should write a book.

Just the other day, my captain was addressing us during our morning meeting, and he started by saying "I don't want to name names or blame anybody, but you guys have to shut the compartment doors." Before he could let out another word, I raised my hand and said he was talking about me. The crew quickly giggled in acceptance, and that was the extent of my shame. The next chapter is about this phenomenon, and how so many people are terrified of public shaming. The days of being hoisted on stage in front of the townsfolk are over, yet we still hold phobias for days past, and this leads to incredible levels of stress —more on that later.

As for leaving compartment doors open, the morning before, as I was leaving the station to end my shift, I grabbed my mask and regulator from the air pack and left the engineers compartment open. This is not usually a big deal, as the operator coming on shift would figure this out while checking off his equipment because he has to walk past this area to get to the driver's seat. But unfortunately, they took a call just after eight, shortly after shift change. Everyone on the crew rushed to the truck, and the operator drove off like a bat out of hell. Also, the trucks have so many warning alarms, he would have had to ignore the one that said stop the truck, on the screen. As I was loading my car to leave, I noticed the ladder truck was parked on the road, and the driver exited the cab and went running behind the truck. About five seconds later, he came back into view carrying two five-gallon buckets (these are full of liquid foam and must have gone tumbling out) while running awkwardly toward the truck. It was hilarious, but I did feel bad and wasted no time taking responsibility the next morning. I even apologized to the driver, and he was not at all upset, but appreciated the contrition.

You see, something magical happens when you do this; the problem goes away. Somewhere along the line people have been convinced and lied to about this. But I have gained nothing but respect by being honest and owning my mistakes. I have been tested many times over by the clouds of karma, and I maintain honesty will set you free. My take is if lying is the only way to maintain your job or whatever you are trying to protect, then it's time to get a different job because it isn't worth omitting virtues. The other important piece of the leadership success puzzle is do not do anything, that despite being honest, will get you into big trouble. This statement should be a no-brainer, but many so-called leaders have done things that are not simply wrong, but illegal, which lead to their career demise. If something feels wrong, it most likely is wrong, so do not do it. We have been gifted with what some call the second brain (our gut) and our inner spirit or guide (conscience), so use them. Make part of your life goal to learn to trust these gifts when they speak to you.

Another aspect of leadership is getting to know the people you lead. For me, it is the Jiu-Jitsu studio. I make it a point to learn and memorize everyone's name as soon as they come through our doors. I then try and learn a little something about them as time goes on. At the end of the day, we all want to feel some level of importance, and for some of my students, the studio is where they can receive that. I do not require my students to call me professor or master, as Rob or coach is fine. But some Jiu-Jitsu black belts require their students to refer to them by formal titles. I prefer a colloquial atmosphere at my studio, but I have been around all types. As a leader at my school, I understand it is my job and responsibility to maintain a good energy and vibe in our space. I also make sure I am still studying and learning the game too, to keep the information I am providing relevant. I believe this is a quality of a good leader. Good leaders are readers, so instead of playing on a phone in front of your crew, pick up a book and encourage those around you to do so as well.

Whether they reach the pinnacle of their career, there is always more to learn and teach. It's also one of the big six rules to success discussed in *Think and Grow Rich*; there are no free lunches and achieving lofty goals requires sacrifice. Hubris is a killer of progress, and leaders are not exempt from its grasp. Speaking of hubris, one more thing I am fond of as a leader is to have a slightly self-deprecating personality —depending on the situation of course.

But anytime I can take the heat for my coaches, I will. Putting your people first is an important role a leader should take.

If you can provide a servant's heart, you can be wildly successful at anything, especially leadership. There is a saying, "*If serving is below you, then leadership is beyond you.*" This is the epitome of good leadership. For example, one of our officers, who is well respected in the department, trains with us and does not expect us to do anything he would not do. Recently, we set up an obstacle course at the station, with challenges purposefully created to make it difficult to save a downed firefighter. I have seen leaders from other departments where they could barely walk from obesity and the ambiguous "bad knees", yet our officer went through the course with us in record time. Also, at mealtimes, he allows everyone else to fix their plates first, and then he fills his. He does not have to do it this way, but he values his people feeling important and not just cogs in the wheel. He also spends most of his time reading, with hopes to be an even better leader —he never stops learning.

I also worked for another officer, earlier in my career that displayed the same values. I had approved leave for my son's award ceremony, and I needed to leave early that day. We ended up on a brush fire, and we were stuck doing cleanup for hours. My officer however, knowing I had a family engagement, sent a fire truck from a different station to pick me up, so I could make my exit on time. Nothing in the policy said he had to provide this service for me, but he made the decision to provide for one of his subordinates because he knew how to lead from his heart. It has been over five years since this day, and the moment is still fresh in my mind.

Another example of great leadership in the department, was an officer I was speaking with recently about a fire he was involved in where the second floor collapsed. This led to a real time mayday situation, and four of our brothers were trapped, including the officer. Two were able to escape quickly, as they had come in together on the first floor, but this officer and another firefighter had fallen through the second floor and were trapped momentarily because of the debris created by the collapsed floor and all the possessions in the home. In speaking with this officer, he stated he understood in the moment, during the mayday, that his mission was to calm the other firefighter down and relay calmness and confidence that they would get out. He also had a moment where he came to terms with his humanity and decided if the other fire fighter could not get out, he would not leave him. In essence, he was willing to die with the other firefighter if that was to be the end; but he also never lost the drive to survive, and thus found a way out for him and his partner. This is the embodiment of leadership. I have to believe most people in this circumstance would not be willing to die and would rather live with the memory of leaving behind a fallen brother. I, and no one else, is in any place to judge somebody if this were the choice to be made, but this officer with serenity and truth in his eyes, displayed the glow of absolute leadership and conviction.

On the flipside however, passive-aggressiveness is the antithesis of good leadership, and never achieves the goal intended. Somewhere along the line we have been convinced that leaving notes and complaining to other people about our concerns is the way to lead, but this is not true. I am quite introverted and try to keep the mood high wherever I go. But, if something needs to be said, I think about how to say it without displaying emotion, and I say it. In Bob Proctor's book, *It's not about the money,* he mentions how most problems are only ten to twenty percent problems, and eighty to ninety percent emotion. Emotion is energy in motion, so the challenge is learning how to control the emotions. All too often, instead of having a conversation to correct or rectify a less than favorable situation, some leaders choose to say nothing and harbor bad energy, and inevitably, this then proliferates through the company. This will work for a while, but eventually the top will blow off and all that suppressed emotion will lead to a blow up or episode of unbalanced emotion.

*Barbara Corcoran,* American business woman and shark on the show *Shark Tank,* believes when someone shows their emotions in business, they are not to be trusted. She was referring to the times people would cry on the show, using sympathy to try and win a deal. I agree. All too often I see officers complain and get emotional when things do not go their way. This is not a good example of leadership.

Early on in my career, I witnessed an officer at our station (different shift) react with emotion. He was told he had to go TDY (which means he will be at another station for the day) for the day. He complained, whined, and eventually took his officer outside to have a conversation about his concerns. All the while, the rest of us were watching and shaking our heads in disappointment. Had it been me, I would have accepted the situation, held my head high, and drove my ass to the station I was assigned to...and if my mood was in the gutter, I would play modern reggae during the drive to raise my vibrations and stop for a tuna sub perhaps. Nothing shows a chink in the armor or a lack of leadership quite like whining and complaining. Doing this at any point, is an example of poor leadership. You only have so much street credit, and once it's depleted, it's very difficult to earn back. Do not allow it to slip away by whining and complaining when things do not go your way. Instead leave temper tantrums to the experts, small children.

Spend time working on yourself, as a leader, before you expect perfection from your subordinates. Be the example you would want to see from your company, and do not get too cocky when you wear the white collar or run things for your business. I have always looked up to and admired the leaders who do not have to tell you how great they are, as their accomplishments speak for them. These are also the same leaders that instead of resting on their laurels once they make rank, continue to improve, and maintain the level of perfection that got them to their lofty goal in the first place.

Humility is also a common characteristic in amazing leaders. *Bob Proctor* says money and wealth are a magnifier. If you were lacking humility prior to achieving wealth, then acquiring wealth will augment your arrogance. I also believe the acquisition of power has the same persuasion over humanity. I have seen it many times over, and heard others complain that people changed when they were promoted. The promotion is not to blame, but people will always have an agenda, whether the agenda is to change the world around them for the better, or prove they are better than everyone else with no regard for others. Unfortunately, there is a spectrum, and money and power give people more rights and choices on said spectrum.

Choose wisely. Remember, the strangers in the building next door do not care about your title, and certainly do not know or care that to a small circle of people, you are their leader. I could wear my jiu-jitsu black belt and kimono out in public, and you know how many people would think I was a karate black belt...many! No one cares. Also, whether you are a kind and well respected leader, or a complete curmudgeon that no one wants to be in the room with, once you retire, you will be forgotten; this is just how it goes. I have seen it happen over and over again, so why not make your time enjoyable and fun. As they say, do not let your success go to your head, and remember where you came from.

# CHAPTER TEN: IGNOMINY

*"If you want to improve, be content to be thought foolish and stupid."*

–EPICTETUS

*"To be yourself in a world that is constantly trying to make you something else is the greatest accomplishment."*

–RALPH WALDO EMERSON

After the fear of poverty or death, I would be willing to place a heavy bet on the fear of failure or being publicly disparaged as the third most common fear that haunts and stifles mankind. Fear of ridicule is one of the main reasons we live in an insipid and homogenous society. We are discouraged from standing out and encouraged to never rock the boat. Manly P. Hall states this regarding the blemish of the education system, *"If one does not become a willing perpetuator of the status quo, then he is an outcast."* We are teased as children when we are different and forced to color and draw within the lines, and we are ostracized as adults when we do not look, talk, or act like everyone else. Oftentimes this comes in the form of reverse ridicule, where we are ridiculed and mocked when we refuse to be part of the gossip circle. Television does a great job of convincing us what is normal or what we should look like, act like and be like. Sports stars, in a way, do the opposite and show us our limitations, which stymies many people's motivation to continue playing sports or remaining active in their adult years because many feel they could not possibly measure up to those who play professionally.

Most people use sports verbally, as their only basis for communicating throughout the day. They talk about not what they are into, or what activities or sports they are involved in, but rather talk about other people that are on their favorite or least favorite teams. Or instead of seeking to join an actual team or athletic minded community, to get some valuable exercise and possibly improve at something, they buy into the idea of modern adulthood and join a fantasy team instead. This is how we "fit in". I never bought into this mode of thinking, not as an adult anyway. As an adult, I wanted more. Thankfully, I found jiu-jitsu. However, in tenth and eleventh grade, I tried vehemently to fit in, but I just could never pull it off. I was different. I am an empath. I feel for and with other people. I enjoyed skateboarding and playing the drums and wrestled for two years in high school. Though I did not know it at the time, I use the right side of my brain which heavily influences emotion, creativity, and the arts. I am also an introvert, so trying to fit in with big crowds has never been easy for me. I can pull it off with aplomb now, as I have made it a lifelong practice to improve this about myself. But given the choice, I prefer a quiet atmosphere with a few good people, or a quiet room with my wife, bulldogs, sons, and a great book. But I do not fear what others think about me. I could never have written this book if I did.

I convince myself that I will make at least one mistake every day and have said this truth in front of others. But therefore, I will be an expert at life (my version of it) someday because I do not fear mistakes. All my posts on social media are positive and have remained that way. I enjoy lifting weights with my sons. My motivation against doing anything is never based on what other people may think. Many moments, during my thirties, were spent on a skateboard, while my sons were riding bikes. Sometimes I would ride with them, on a BMX bike. A few times, other adults (often old ladies) would mistake me for one of them, often by yelling at the young men for not stopping at stop signs and such from their BMW's. As a side note, it really is a challenge to be a kid these days. Adults are always in such a hurry, are rattled by stress and have no patience for youth on bicycles, scooters or in general. It's quite sad. There were no other dads outside on skateboards; in fact, I have never seen another dad out on a skateboard or bike (with their children) in town ever, and we have been living in a small town, with plenty of flat terrain, since 2008. The point I am trying to make is akin to the quote by George Bernard Shaw, "*We don't stop playing because we grow old; we grow old because we stop playing.*" Do not be afraid to be seen having fun and doing things that others might think frivolous or beneath them.

Relentless positivity is not something many people strive to have, I have found. Recently, it had been raining for about three weeks straight, and it was February in Virginia. Our new packaged A/C-Heat pump unit was getting challenged by the ice-cold rain. I had to go outside with warm water, every few hours, to thaw the fan or it would damage the motor. I am not sure this is the best way to quell the problem, but it was the weekend and seemed like the best option. It worked. As I was in the grocery store, the store clerk mentioned how gloomy and miserable it was, and I could not help but retort with how I was still grateful to be here...and I meant it. It would have been easy to "fit in" and complain, as it always is when something is not what most deemed fun or exciting, but I do not feel that way anymore. Even a busy night with no sleep on the medic, is not enough to tank my positivity. Because of this, I genuinely believe we are meant to learn gratitude as a lesson during our human experience. Instead, most people complain to connect with others or to express themselves. This does not have to be the social norm.

Speaking of positivity or mood enhancement, when I was in the fire academy, my academy mates and I had to carry a piece of rope and water bottle with us everywhere we went. One of my buds left his rope lying about, more than once, and the instructors threatened to fire him for it. To say morale was low because of this was an understatement. To help boost the mood and "take one for the team" I decided I would perform our morning PT in my wrestling singlet the next morning, so I did. The singlet was the one I wore in high school, and I was now a 31-year-old man. Luckily, I had not gained much weight or accumulated much fat in the previous thirteen years, but the unitard was quite revealing. The visual was quite funny, and the entire fire academy got a great laugh out of the experience.

When the instructors saw what I was doing, they understood why I was doing it, and could not help but laugh as well. They also threatened to make us run, more than we ever had in our lives, if I ever wore it again; I never did, but I accomplished my goal to embarrass myself to boost the morale of my crew. It felt awesome. The captain (now chief) during the academy still brings this moment up, when we get to talking about the good old days. If I cared what people really thought about me, I never would have had the courage to try this stunt. Instead, it brought some much-needed humor to our lives during a stressful time.

Most days, I prefer to wash my truck or lift weights, and often in short shorts, in my garage when I am home. It is a freeing feeling when you do not care what people think about you. One day, a few years ago, my wife and I went out for a bike ride, and we took my mother-in laws' Yorkie. I have a Haro BMX bike, so I strapped one of those square milk crates to my handlebars with a bunch of zip ties. I padded the crate and put her yorkie in it. It was summertime, so I was wearing short shorts and a straw hat. My wife rode with me too. She was riding an adult sized bike. It was hilarious how many dudes in lifted trucks stared at us —kind of makes you wonder. Had I cared about fitting in, little moments like this would never happen. One of my favorite statements on this topic is "Dare to be different. Dare to be you."

Speaking of short shorts, I began wearing them about four or five years ago, and my son thought I was an old stooge, and again different (I do not shave my legs like many men do these days, but I also do not skip leg day). Not long after, all the fellas his age and slightly older were wearing them — go figure.

Life is meant to be lived, and you should not be afraid to live outside the box. If people talk about you, it is because they see something in themselves that is lacking. Also, just about everyone will talk about you at some point. Who cares? It's their breath and energy going to waste, not yours. Independence is something most people will truly never accomplish, as it requires thinking for yourself or being what is dubbed a free thinker. Most people have been relegated to a few choices about what they are going to wear, talk like or even think like. This phenomenon has been labeled "group-think".

Take the masks for example. At some point, everyone just wanted to fit in. Most were not willing or even cared enough to talk about the root of the problem, our food choices, eating habits and sedentary lifestyle in a country where food comes fast and at the expense of quality and health. Instead, let us all show how much we care by covering our mouths with a piece of cloth. Some even wore two masks, further complicating their ability to perfuse their body with a fresh supply of oxygen. I cannot help but wonder what kind of regrets most people will have when they are reminiscing on their deathbed. I am sure most will wish they had tried to be different, with no regard for how others viewed them. As they say, at the end of the day, who cares.

When I quit the team of the jiu-jitsu organization that awarded me my black belt, I was scared and nervous, as I was leaving behind a chapter of my life that was seven years of work and effort. But I was no longer enjoying being a part of that team, and hardly knew most of the people on the team anymore; the leaders of the team often utilized the term "family" when referring to the group, but most of us had a very superficial understanding of those we shared the mats with. This is not necessarily a bad thing, but I found fault with such "lofty labels" and terms. I have never used the word family around my students, though I have formed some amazing friendships with many. I have kissed a few of the menfolk on the forehead after watching them give their all during competition and told quite a few I love them; this is no distortion of the truth.

Prior to leaving that organization, I had come to an epiphany that I did not fit it with the vibe, and it was time to move on. I did not know it at the time, but I needed more depth and room to be creative in my jiu-jitsu journey. The group I left behind shunned me, or at least that was what they thought they did. I never looked back and told none of the other students I was leaving, as I did not want to set the tone that I wanted to take any students from that organization.

Not long after opening the doors to our gym, some of the unsettled members, in the previous group, kicked the tires about leaving too, but I never solicited them. Eventually a few did leave and realized there is life after death —death meaning leaving behind a part of your life you thought you needed but was pulling you down more than pushing you forward. Some even complained about the treatment they were receiving at other places, but admitted they lacked the courage to leave. For me, this endeavor was a big experience in creating my destiny and being intensely empowered because of it.

Do you think Einstein cared about fitting in, or Elon Musk? Not at all. Fitting in would have meant mediocrity, and neither of those amazing people are mediocre. I do not allow my "inner critic" as mentioned in the book *Limitless* by Kwik, or my "drunk monkey" as mentioned in the book *Quiet Mind Epic Life* by Ferry control me or stop me from having a great time in life. This voice comes from within, and it is the voice of the ego. Once you learn to put the ego in its place, you will control your destiny.

Here is a beautifully articulated quote by John Foster, "*When a firm, decisive spirit is recognized it is curious to see how the space clears around a man and leaves him space and freedom.*" Napoleon Hill (How to Own Your Own Mind) goes on to say, "*I have observed many times, by watching a determined man who knew where he was going, as he walked down the street. I have actually seen people look back over their shoulders, become confused, and quickly sidestep out of his way. The determined mind projects an influence that is felt by everyone within its range. His presence makes itself felt.*" This is proof life not only rewards the risk takers, but also bends and correlates to their energy. It may feel lonely at first, when you decide to be different, act different and become a free-thinking human, but eventually your moxy and courage will pay off. It certainly has for us. Bet on yourself and go out and live your best life. You may only get to experience you this one time. Do not waste it!

I end this chapter with the following quote about what is "normal", and if this is what it means to be normal, maybe it's time to try a little weird or abnormal every once in a while.

*"Normal is getting dressed in clothes that you buy for work and driving through traffic in a car you are still paying for in order to get to the job you need to pay for the clothes and car and the house you leave vacant all day so you can afford to live in it."*

—ELLEN GOODMAN

# CHAPTER ELEVEN: GRATITUDE

*"Everything comes to you in the right moment.*
*Be patient. Be grateful."*

—BUDDHA

*"Remember your average day is someone else's miracles manifested;*
*don't forget to appreciate the humble moments."*

—ROBERT LOY

You must have an attitude of gratitude. The cup is either half empty or half full. Your cup must be overflowing before you can pour into someone else's. See the world through rose colored glasses. These are just a few platitudes about gratitude, but there are plenty more. When we read these things, it seems so simple to keep a good attitude and remain grateful, yet so many people struggle with being happy and grateful. Why? First, one must realize most of us have been given everything we will ever need to be successful in this life. If you believe the big bang brought us here, and there is no higher power, fine...it makes no difference. But God made just about everyone the same —two eyes, ears, arms, legs, and brain; you get the point.

The wealthiest person in the world was born with the same parts and potential as the poorest. God or the universe does not drop us off at the doorstep of life and say, good luck, you will need it sucker. No, we were gifted with everything we will ever need to achieve greatness and happiness, only most of us will never learn or accept we have what it takes to be successful because we buy into the negativity all around us; we allow our limiting beliefs to stop us from achieving greatness.

Why do you think children, no matter what their financial situation is, find joy in play and imagination? Even in third world countries, you will find children outside playing in the dirt and utilizing their imagination to emulate their favorite comic book hero or maybe an astronaut. They have not allowed others, circumstances or the fear of ignominy coerce this love for life out of them; essentially, they are still living internally, and not allowing exterior forces to change their perception. One of the absolute best ways to overcome the white noise of society's ills, is to live, breathe and spread gratitude. There are so many drugs on the market for "fixing" anxiety and depression. During the 2020 circus, I saw a huge increase in patients with anxiety and mental illness. Each person had something in common, they all had the bodies and mind to keep going, but they chose to give in to the hurt and fear. According to The Devil in *Outwitting the Devil,* by *Napoleon Hill,* only two percent of the population will be awake or driven by love, and therefore not hindered by fear. I consider myself part of this small community. This does not mean that I fear nothing. Like most human beings, I have many fears and phobias, but the difference is, I do not allow fear to control me or make my decision for me. For years I was accelerating through my life on hope and ambition, unaware that I was forgoing fear as a motivation. For instance, when my wife and I decided to move our family three hours south and start a contracting business during the 2008 recession, my father was against it because he was afraid for me and my family. He believed this would be a bad financial move for my family, as did others. At the time, this endeavor meant my wife would be leaving a secure career with the federal government. But I did not have this fear, or rather, I did not listen to the voice that tries to deny us the experience of taking chances in our life. Instead, I silenced the voice and thought of all the potential that was waiting for us in our new area, and the feelings of this reality allowed me to be grateful. I was grateful that we could so easily unroot and start over with a hope and a dream, but I had to quiet the voice of limitation and fear.

This dubious voice is the ego, and it is a record that never stops playing if you allow it to remain in control. It's the same voice in our heads that tries to convince us we are not good enough, tall enough, loud enough, rich enough and on and on. But, because I have had the courage to take so many risks in my life, I cannot help but overflow with gratitude, and abundance. I am grateful that I did not settle for working for someone else. I am grateful I have struggled during my thirties, so no matter what, I have decided to live stress free in my forties and beyond. During my studies of the law of attraction, the theory of gratitude was a huge concept. I kept, and still do, a daily wish list or journal to help me stay humble, hungry, and grateful. There would be three columns I would write on the page.

In one column, I would write a few things I was grateful for that day. Then I would have a column for what I hoped the universe would bring to me, and the last column would be my goal or something I would accomplish for the day. This has, and continues to, lead to some amazing moments, experiences, and things to manifest in my life.

Now, even if I do not write in the actual journal, I still think about and appreciate the many things I am grateful for. In the beginning, this can be a challenge, as we are not programmed or encouraged to be grateful. Unfortunately, you do not see much in the way of modeling gratitude from others. In a world of sales, marketing and bad news, literally around every corner, it is easier to wallow and settle into our own misery than to appreciate the little things in life. We should not have to be like the cancer thrivers referenced in *Things No One Else Can Teach Us, by Humble the Poet*, to appreciate how much beauty and magnificence there is in the world. The ladies in his book began to appreciate the simplicity and beauty a reflection in a pond can bring, when they were fighting cancer. Because oftentimes, when we are reminded of how ephemeral life really is, we stop and appreciate all the little things that we overlook when we are focused on the rat race. The sky is also a reminder of how beautiful life really is. I gaze at the sky daily and take in the splendor of this life. At night, I often sit amongst the stars and gaze upward in immense gratitude. This is the way to fast track your dream life —give gratitude to God and the universe.

> *"Whatever is true, whatever is noble, whatever is right,*
> *whatever is pure, whatever is lovely, whatever is admirable*
> *—think about such things."*

> **(PHIL 4:8)**

It is also very lonely to be one of the two percent, in the beginning. I agree with the thought that you must be comfortable hanging out with yourself first before you can really understand how to show your true self to others. You could see it during the 2020 circus, people wearing their masks and displaying worn eyes and hunched posture from allowing the box on the wall or their phones to convince them the world was burning. Most looked like newly turned zombies. I asked people, have you seen more hearses on the road? Have you seen anyone keeled over coughing in the last eight months? Have you been to the ER to see for yourself if it's really the image of chaos and gnashing of teeth, as the media so vividly animates? Being an FTO, on the medic every other day of our cycle (which equates to an average of thirty to forty visits to the ER for transport a month) I had an answer for all of this, Hell No! But, even if all the above was true, wouldn't it make sense to remain strong and appreciate the fact that you still have a chance, and your heart is still beating?

It is said without darkness there could be no light, so doesn't it make sense to push the agenda of gratitude because of all the people who were still standing after the Virus? This is not to say the lives lost during all of this were not tragic, as they certainly were, but unlike most people with loud opinions in the world, I had seen behind the truth curtain for many years.

I had taken many calls at retirement homes that were full of drug addled, forgotten souls, where their "caretakers" could not remember the last time the patient was seen normal, or they had just come on shift. Now because a Virus was putting them out of their unrealized misery, everyone was in an uproar. The irony was these souls were still dying alone, in their beds, as before the 2020 Circus, so nothing had really changed for these pitiful forgotten souls. Well, truthfully, now they were waiting longer to receive care because of all the equipment we had to use and don to keep us and them "safe". So, theirs and everyone's chances of survival were curtailed because of the aforementioned change in our care protocols. Because I am still strong, and not imprisoned in any place like this, I am grateful.

I am grateful I am strong, mentally, and physically. I am grateful I have a woman at home that loves me. I am grateful for mobility, and that I can use the restroom on my own (I have had many patients who cannot do this because of certain illnesses) and feed myself. Last week while on a medic call, we had a patient that was my age, and bedridden with a colostomy bag, so I am grateful that being forty does not mean the same existence for everyone. Again, God gave me all the tools I need to be successful at birth, and so the gratitude list goes on and on. I am grateful I discovered modern reggae and chillstep music to help keep my vibrations strong when driving and hanging at the station because imbibing audible positivity is as important as visual and ethereal imbibement, though we have more control over what we take in audibly.

Every Morning when the coffee touches my lips, I am grateful. There is a saying, win the morning, win the day. If you can wake up with a positive mindset, and begin your day strong, you can generate many great things during your day through momentum and eventually a paradigm shift toward the positive. I am genuinely grateful the minute I wake up in the morning because I have mobility, working plumbing, a home that surrounds and protects me, and a wife next to me that loves me, two young strong sons to carry the name —the list goes on and on. When I am walking outside to drive my jeep to work, I look up at the sky and say thank you. I set my alarm in the morning, so I have enough time to relax and enjoy my alone time before beginning my day.

Instead of starting my day thinking about lack, like most people —you know, thinking I only have so much time for this or that, or I must hurry up and leave so I can beat traffic. Instead, I have almost an hour before I must depart for work, and I still arrive thirty minutes early every day. I am grateful that my commute is only 20 minutes. I am grateful if I want something from the store, I can go and buy it. I am grateful for all my many freedoms and take none for granted. Making a point to display gratitude in public goes a long way by saying please and thank you when someone does something for you —this is also called manners, but gratitude has a certain ring to it. Again, if you start by winning the morning, you can win the day. I try to remain grateful from the time I lift my head in the morning until I lay it down at night. If a negative thought enters my head, I try my best to cancel it with a positive thought filled with gratitude.

Overtime, this becomes easier, as you begin to tune into all the positives in your life, the negative force in your life will lose strength. True gratitude is appreciating all the luxuries we take for granted, like running water, the ability to play our favorite music, or go outside for a walk with a friend. Gratitude is like a muscle; it must be exercised daily or it will atrophy. If you find it difficult to acknowledge the positives, it may take some work at first, but I promise you, you will eventually realize how good life is and how many positives are everywhere. Throughout the day, there will be roadblocks and lessons learned, but the key to mastering the game of life is to remain grateful and enjoy the journey. Try and learn something new or create something new as often as you can. Once you begin to embrace all the wonders of the world and everything the world has to offer, be grateful, and give gratitude to the creator, as it will come back to you tenfold. I am grateful you chose to read my book. Thank you.

# CHAPTER TWELVE: THE IRON

*"The Iron never lies to you. You can go outside and listen to all kinds of talk, get told you are a god or a total bastard. The iron will always kick you the real deal. The iron is the great reference point, the all-knowing perspective giver."*

**—HENRY ROLLINS**

There is a scene in the movie *40-Year-Old Virgin* where Steve Carrells character goes speed dating, and he is sitting across from a woman named Gina (she pronounces it like vagina, but minus the va). She tells him he is very pretty, real soft and has delicate features, and basically wants to dress him up like a woman because it would be an easy sell and fun, according to her. There are loads of men in the world who may someday have this encounter, and it is often because they do not know the iron. There is also a meme that you can google, and it's a picture of Arnold with his shit eating grin, while pointing his finger saying, *"Your dad doesn't lift, then happy Mother's Day to your dad."* Does this sound like something a toxic male would say, maybe; but it is also somewhat true and perhaps a little bit facetious. I do not agree that if you do not lift you are not manly, but others have made the above statements to playfully rib the non-lifters; so unfortunately, the sentiment and opinion does exist.

Of course, let us not forget about the commercials for a certain fitness center that belittles those that pick up heavy objects and put them down; I never quite understood the problem with people who enjoy lifting heavy things. If anyone ever did a ride along with the fire department or an EMS unit, they would see the people that fall down and need to be picked up are rarely under three hundred pounds, and they are usually naked —which tends to complicate things even further. Obviously, this also means someone must have the horsepower to pick up the zaftig grandma or uncle, and it's not the string bean looking fella in the back that does not possess the capacity to trip the "lunk alarm". Please do not think I am picking on the little guy, but facts are facts and well physics are physics. Because of this undeniable fact, I look at lifting primarily as injury prevention and the fountain of youth.

I must single handedly give so much credit to the iron. I will never forget watching Arnold Schwarzenegger, when I was a little twerp about ten or eleven years of age and wanting to be just like him. When terminator two came out, I was in love with two things, the movie, and the soundtrack. *You Could be Mine* by *Guns & Roses* was my favorite song that year. Arnold's book *The Encyclopedia of Modern Bodybuilding* is incredible. Every man should own this book, and every father should have a copy of this book at home to bestow to their children when they are old enough to experience the iron. When I was in my teens and early twenties, I had a subscription to *Muscle and Fitness*. I would use the workouts and suggestions in the magazine to steer my monthly workouts, or just use them as supplementation to what I was already doing in the weight room. Even with modern information streams like Instagram and YouTube, you should support and own the classics.

I started my weight room journey when I was around ten years old. We had a set of plastic weights that were full of sand. They were dumbbells, all of five pounds. I did arm work every day until my dad explained how the muscle building process works, which then I did arm work every other day. My father always had weights and a killer drum set when I was growing up. He had a loft above the garage, and he had a weight bench with loads of free weights. From watching my dad, I decided to learn how to play drums and lift weights. I also remember a guy in our high school that was yoked to the gills, would workout with his uncles, and I recall thinking how awesome this was. As for the weights, I have been lifting consistently since high school. I started with the basic stuff, bench, curls, and triceps extensions. Eventually I discovered deadlifts and squats. Pull Ups were impossible when I first attempted to learn, but after a few months, I was able to do sets of ten. These would remain a staple in my lifting regimen for my entire life, as well as deadlifts.

A buddy of mine, who we refer to as the Greek God, as he is built like *Artemus Dolgin,* during a conversation at the fire station, he recommended taking creatine. I used to take creatine, but once I had taken the full amount (roughly a month's worth) I would stop for many months or sometimes a year. After my friend told me that creatine monohydrate is the most studied supplement, and it does no harm, I decided to use it more often. I still cycle off quite frequently but enjoy the benefit it provides. I have tried my best to research it on my own but kept finding conflicting opinions. Male pattern baldness was one of the side effects some websites were claiming, but the Greek God had a full head of thick hair, as did many other users that I know. Plus, I am already mostly bald, so no worries here. As I mentioned in the handyman chapter, my buddy is a maven in the health industry and fitness coach, so I trust his opinion as an expert in his craft, over all the conflicting white noise Google has to offer. Other than protein shakes most days, I take nothing else. I have never imbibed pre workout, as I come from the days before there was pre workout; we had *Ultimate Orange,* and that concoction was disgusting but effective.

Because of deadlifts and squats, I have always been one of the stronger guys. When I did my fire fighter physical entry exam, the last station we had to complete was the drummy drag. This dummy was around 180 pounds of dead weight, and to me, felt light as a feather. The proctor that was the safety during the drag told me I pulled it the fastest he had ever seen. Another time my strength came in handy in the fire service, when I was precepting at the station, the guys set up an obstacle course in the bunk room with a firefighter down scenario. To challenge me, they had our Lieutenant, who was 6'4 and every bit of 375 pounds, act as the victim. I got through the challenge in good time and grabbed him and slid him to safety with ease. They gave me an attaboy for that accomplishment. They also never questioned my strength again after this performance.

When I was going through the fire academy, we had to be at the academy by six thirty am, as our PT would begin at seven. I had not been a morning person at this point, but I made sure to be at the gym by five thirty every morning to have my time with the iron. Because of the iron, there was nothing I could not physically do or figure out during the months at the academy, and because of the mental fortitude it takes to continue a long-term relationship with the iron, I was mentally strong and capable too. I owe this and a good deal of my reputation as a man to the iron. I also owe the iron endless gratitude, because at 40 years young, I have no injuries or lingering pains and have never needed surgeries (jiu-jitsu and the iron have made this possible) or required chiropractic intervention; though I have gone to a chiropractor a few times, but nothing regular. I have had conversations with other firemen, younger than me, that have written themselves off as over the hill and not interested in improving their physicality; this is madness.

With the iron, I strengthen the bigger, obvious muscles, and jiu-jitsu allows me to strengthen the smaller, intrinsic muscles —it's the perfect combination. The iron has also given me a body that I can rely on, and thus has provided me the opportunity to continue to try new things and have many hobbies. Also, while everyone was running scared from the Virus, I held the opinion that I would be alright, and still do. Infact, I improved my diet and gained even more balance in my life during the last year.

I have met so many men who doubt themselves and lack confidence because they put no time into improving themselves physically. There are many men I have known that did nothing to enhance themselves physically but believe themselves to be superior men because of their intellect. Because of this imbalance, they are only able to achieve so much because of what their bodies are not able to do. To be balanced and efficient, we need to take care of our mind, body, heart and soul. Obviously with so many obese and sick people, they have made the choice to ignore the body aspect. I have also seen many injuries occur because people lack the strength and stability that muscle provides.

There are other ways to lift heavy things and gain a workout if weights are not your thing. For example, for a while I had a large tire at home, that was around 475 lbs. I would often raise it, flip it and do other types of workouts. I have never torn or damaged anything or needed to stop lifting for more than a few days from non-serious injuries, and because of this I have nothing but love and gratitude for the iron. Also, I will cycle in body weight work with gymnastic rings quite often to keep variety in my workouts.

Again, It is the reason I am forty going on twenty. I have conversations all the time with friends who do not lift, and they are always dealing with back and neck pain...sometimes other areas too. A few friends have had to take time off from work for tweaking their backs doing mundane things like step-ping out of their vehicle or picking up their laundry, and these same friends do not have a relationship with the iron. I am pain free. I can feel when I have not lifted a certain body part, especially my shoulders. If I neglect to work them, or lose track of their day in the rotation, they will start to feel sore, as if they are calling out to me. Other friends who live by the iron agree with this feeling, as they feel it too. With the Iron, you develop a deeper understand-ing and friendship with your own body. If something begins to feel different, I can always track it to a new workout, or a day missed in the weight room.

Flexibility is huge with lifting too. Anyone I have studied in the weight-lifting world, aside from the freaky huge roided types, all use stretching to enhance muscle growth. I avoided stretching for many years but have since realized it's value and need for daily recovery. Gordon Ryan, who is the best no-gi grappler in the world, and an iron addict, also preaches the importance of stretching, but do not take my word for it. In the book *Game Changers* by Dave Asprey, he interviewed a successful biohacker and strength and condi-tioning educator named Charles Poliquin. According to Poliquin, strength training and stretching is more beneficial for your brain health than long distance aerobic exercise; basically put, weightlifting, and stretching have proved more favorable for people suffering from Parkinson's —he provides data to back this up in his book.

Also, in the book *Tools of Titans, by Tim Ferriss,* among the many of his interviews was with a strength and flexibility coach named Christopher

Sommer. He mentioned how he did a mobility seminar for big and power-ful lifters, mainly plyometric exercises, and the bigger they were, the quicker they fell. Most could not make it through the warm-up (not unlike when we have guests in jiu-jitsu class), so this is proof, stretching and floor work is a necessary evil, if you really want to epitomize strength. Also, because stretch-ing, and strength and conditioning work has been studied and proven to be beneficial for your long term mental and physical health, for all those jokers that like to castigate those that pick things up and put them down, you might want to start picking things up yourself soon.

I will stretch after my workouts and before practicing jiu-jitsu. This has been a game changer for me and will probably lead to a future of Yoga practice. My wife and I understand the importance of yoga and have begun bartering with a great yoga instructor in exchange for a membership at our gym. She teaches yoga once a week at our studio for free tuition. But for now, stretching daily has slowed down the aging clock once again. If you need help with what to stretch or how to, there are many good YouTube videos available for your needs, as well as countless online articles and books about the subject. There is also a great YouTube channel called *Yoga for BJJ*, which caters a bit more to jiu-jitsu practitioners. Or you could join a gym and schedule some personal training sessions, with an emphasis and heavy interest in stretching.

Stress, as most of us know, is a silent killer (though it has amplified it's bark quite substantially in the last year), and most think there is no way to stop or curtail its powers. The Iron will prove this is fractured thinking. Aside from jiu-jitsu, the Iron is my second favorite form of self-improvement and therapy. The Iron will never lie to you and compliment you for substandard efforts, so it will always be a relationship based on honesty and hard work. As a man, I appreciate this, and crave this relationship. It also, like jiu-jitsu, gives me a goal that I can never break or overcome. There will always be a surplus of weights, sitting on the floor, staring at me to remind me that I have improvements to make, much like the many techniques and theories in jiu-jitsu that I have yet to master; therefore one of favorite axioms is a black belt is a white belt that never quit, or just a dirty white belt...take your pick. Climbing this kind of mountain, where there will never be a reachable summit, will always allow me goals and activity to keep my mind and body young. What a great addiction too!

When I wake up, and finish my morning routine, I am typically excited to get into the weight room. At the station, we have a great weight room with plenty of iron, which only a small few of us utilize. I have a great gym set up in my garage, and I am a member at a small gym, near my home. During the Virus, I wanted to support a small gym, and purchased memberships for my entire family. My son, who is now 14, also understands the importance of the iron. He has two buddies that often come over to our house to lift with my son. Oftentimes people place a diminutive value on their fitness and mental health. The pharmaceutical industry is a billion-dollar industry, and the mental health sector would not be so lucrative if people could learn how to control and win the game of life. I believe the Iron provides an important piece to the mental wellness puzzle. The other advantage the iron provides is the desire to get stronger and look better. This often leads to better eating habits.

According to a study by the World Health Organization, worldwide obesity has nearly tripled since 1975. In 2016, more than 1.9 billion adults were overweight and of those, 650 million adults were deemed obese; this equates to thirty nine percent of the world population being overweight. Often, people have succumbed to the notion that there is a pill for just about everything and forget that real medicine is staring them in the face every time they visit the grocery store. It's called food. Food is medicine; it is a nutraceutical and acts upon the body's many systems and receptors either positively or negatively. We are inundated with ads for candy, sugary drinks, packaged and processed pseudo-food and medicines that require a doctor's prescription. But you can still purchase frozen or fresh vegetables with no additives, organic meats and cheeses, almond milk and so on. The companies that sell the "good stuff" do not spend billions on ads. When was the last time you saw an ad for broccoli or mixed vegetables?

Sadly, it is not entirely society's fault, as there is clearly a war on the human body and human health. We have been told, and encouraged by the media that being obese is normal and healthy, and chemicals are not helping —over 93 percent of the corn and soy produced in this country are genetically modified, thus we become modified when we consume these Frankenfoods. Just look at pictures of our grandparents compared to our generation; it is quite alarming. Also, Monsanto, the company that owned Round-Up and recently purchased by Bayer, is responsible for a large quantity of the world's food supply. But despite this seemingly obvious monopoly, we still have a choice to look for and demand fresh crops, meat, and poultry.

Just the other day I was meeting my family at a fast-food restaurant (their choice), and they were discussing the pricing difference between their two favorite fast food restaurants and mentioned they had experienced a mild stomach ache days earlier from eating at yet another semi-fast food restaurant. These same family members were like most and extremely pro mask and pro vaccine thinkers, in their belief system. The irony was that this same-day, I had picked up over seventeen packages of grass-fed ground beef and a dozen fresh eggs from my neighbor who has chickens. I had not eaten any of the food my family were talking about in years, yet I was stuck in their world like most —the unhealthy "they have a pill or that" world. As for those that enjoy copious amounts of fast food, it is no wonder nearly forty percent of the population has made the choice to stop eating healthy, as they have been convinced junk food and medication prescriptions are reality. Thankfully, the Iron has encouraged me to have balance, and keep a consistent diet.

I cannot say the Iron would be the elixir the world would need to end such problems, but I do believe it offers a more natural and goal-oriented solution. The people I have met in the weight room tend to be happier and calmer, at least from appearances. The iron gives lifters a real time, real world, analysis of progress or failure. Therefore, no outside source is needed to seek improvement. Also, the people I have met that have admitted to taking drugs to help control their emotions and curtail depression, are not typically members of a gym and do not challenge themselves in that environment consistently. To the iron I say thank you from the heart, thank you. Because of you, I will always be strong, healthy and have goals to keep my mind and body focused and moving forward. Also, I will remain masculine, and physically capable which matters greatly to me. Thank you!

# CHAPTER THIRTEEN:
# WASTED TIME

*"Once a nation of zombies has been created, the population must be kept docile and under control. Many commentators have written about how so many Americans become zombielike while sitting mesmerized before their TVs for more than eight hours a day."*

**— JIM MARRS, THE TRILLION DOLLAR CONSPIRACY**

Not too long ago, I would spend hours staring at my phone dealing with the ebb and flow of emotions that are associated with all my social media friends and their various drama and situations. A handful of these friends I have never met, and most likely never will. This goes double for Instagram followers...kind of interesting that we place such a high value on the avatars in our life, no? This nascent glimpse of reality rings even more loudly for those with a huge number of followers and Facebook friends —pseudo celebrities if you will.

After a day invested in the social media wasteland, I would feel the pulse of anxiety running through my cells and also wonder where the time went. I had accomplished nothing and done nor created anything. I saw a study that most people spend around two to three hours a day on social media (this does not even include television lazy person time), and I would be willing to bet that most would agree this is a modest estimate. When you include the time you are on the toilet, eating meals and sleeping, the time you have left to accomplish anything useful or learn something new becomes nonexistent.

That time does not seem important now perhaps, but what about when you are in your 80s, and begin to see the last few granules of sand falling through the hourglass. Or how about this time paradox —what if it was your very last day on this earth? Would you want to waste it staring at a screen then? We have become a distracted and narcotized society. I see it anytime I am out in public, or anywhere these days really.

I have seen some good and accomplished men choose to spend their prime daylight hours staring at their cell phones. I have had more conversations than I like to admit where the person I was talking to was only able to engage in the conversation in small pieces. They were not able to turn off their addiction long enough to have an adult conversation... like a full-sized child that needs his binky. I too was beginning to form an addiction with my phone to this level before realizing something had to change. For example, during a typical conversation with said people, me or someone else would-be mid-sentence and they would have to look at their phone, which led us to believe they were no longer listening or wanting to be a part of the conversation. They would do their best to multitask, but it is never enjoyable talking to the top of someone's head. Because of this occurrence, I have become more selective who I give my time to and have conversations with. I not only avoid people who cannot place their phone in their pocket for more than five minutes, but I also avoid negative people. They are a time suck too. They are the energy vampires that the former monk *Dandapani* talks about. Succinctly put, he states we only have so much energy, and energy vampires will suck the energy out of you via their negativity. Naturally, wherever we place our focus, we place our energy.

If energy cannot be created or destroyed, then we only have a certain amount each day, and where your focus goes your energy flows. Most of us know the feeling...we hang out with the certain friend that always must unload their woes on us. We listen intently and offer our input, only to be exhausted once the conversation is over. This is of course assuming you are an empathetic person. A good friend should be there to help you recover from a bad experience or ruined relationship, and this is a small act of service —which is good. But this should not be the only way the friendship goes. At some point, it's unfair to expect your friends to continue to listen to your woes. It goes back to the common saying "why complain. No one would listen anyway." Exactly! This is true.

I recently saw a study by the *Pew Research Center*, that a quarter of the population does not read at all, and according to a study, 24 percent admitted to not having read anything electronic or hard copy in over a year. I don't think I need to do any research to find out how many Americans spend their time looking at their phones, crushing candies and being hypnotized by social media. I was recently speaking to a mother of one of our youth students, and I asked what her eleven-year-old son wanted for Christmas. She said he wanted a phone, and he was probably going to get it. She seemed a bit reluctant as if she knew the addiction habits that would follow.

A friend of mine, whose son is now 18, had to be sent to military school because when the son was 16, my friend tried to take his phone away to punish him. The son's addiction was so real and embedded, that when he grabbed his phone, the son lunged at my friend and attempted to attack him. The experience was quite frightening, as the son was full size and appeared to be in a rage induced trance during the attack. This is a real dilemma when an addiction culminates in violence against another, especially a family member. Originally it was television that was the main mind melting device, but now phones reign supreme. They really should not be called phones anymore, as that is the feature used the least.

Scientists have said that soon after watching television, your brain induces low alpha waves, which are associated with low meditative states or daydreaming which is usually a desirable place to be, but when watching television, you become susceptible to what you are imbibing. In a low alpha wave state, you are no longer thinking with your conscious mind but allowing your subconscious mind to control the influx of information you receive, so your ability to filter information is greatly curtailed. Another interesting find, is that our subconscious mind is capable of processing roughly eleven million bits of sensory data per second, as opposed to only fifty bits by our conscious mind. And according to Jim Kwik in the book Limitless, he basically says our brains are not meant to hold onto so much useless information. We lower our guard or allow a breach to our inherent firewall when we watch too much television, and those that create the various programs we watch know this! —Hence the never-ending late night and early morning infomercials, as that is the time to "capture" the audience. With an overabundance of television, you become lazy couch zombies without even the motivation to look for a good meal of brains.

During the Film *Awake,* David Icke (not everything he says is so out there) mentions a top-secret document (of unknown origin) found on a copier in 1986, and subsequently published titled *Silent Weapons for Quiet Wars.* The document recommends and provides many suggestions for social engineering which eerily correlate with how mainstream society is trending today. One of the "suggestions" on entertainment was to keep the public entertainment below a sixth-grade level. Case in point, have you seen the shows the masked dancer or masked singer? It's absolute vacuous nonsense and holds no tangible value. The contestants dress up like food and sing and perform, while the celebrities clap and celebrate frivolously while judging the food inspired singers.

It proves the point of television when not dispelling bad news is to keep us distracted and mindlessly entertained. People act like they worship celebrities and sports stars, more than anything else; it is idolatry at it's finest. This is often the highlight of most people's day, after work and family obligation, to sit and watch television.

*"Football, beer and above all gambling, filled up the horizons of their minds. To keep them in control was not difficult."*

—GEORGE ORWELL 1984

It is no wonder most people suffer from laziness, chronic back pain, hypertension, heart disease and other illnesses brought on by sedentary lifestyle; oh right, and this is also why we imprisoned our society during 2020 to preserve and protect everyone's right to continue this modus operandi. Spending large amounts of free time staring at screens also keeps people in a low vibrational state, and considering we are all part of infinite intelligence, and God most likely chooses to experience his creation through us, this means the creator must endure the garbage we imbibe with our senses.

To put it another way, most people would agree that God is omniscient, but what does that mean? According to astrophysicist Bernard Haisch, in the book *The God Theory,* he speaks candidly about our interconnectedness with God and offers the idea that whatever we choose to experience, God gets to experience. With free will, we have the choice to continue in our low vibrational state, and so many of us do make this choice. There is something very wrong with this, and there are consequences.

During a conversation the other day, my friend who works in the ICU said he has seen a huge increase in stroke admissions the last few months. You know what causes most strokes...the effects of high blood pressure and long-term stress. Too much exposure to media and negativity will typically do one of two things (or both), desensitize, and stress the observer. Coincidentally, stroke was the most debilitating illness and second leading cause of death in 2019 —second only to heart disease, which is also caused by uncontrolled and high levels of stress.

I wrote a goal card a few months before beginning this book, and one of the goals was to stay off social media and read more books. The end goal was I wanted to have more time to be creative. It took some time to gain momentum, but eventually I removed Facebook off my phone and only checked Instagram once a day for around five minutes. I made sure this goal card stayed in my wallet, and I read the goal card every day. In the book, The Greatest Secret in The World, the first "scroll" or goal the reader must accomplish is the forming of better habits. If you are interested in setting goals for yourself and tapping into your own creativity, I highly recommend you watch the YouTube video called *Create Something by Christian Graugart.* He is a BJJ black belt who created the *BJJ Globetrotters,* and he travels the world hosting jiu-jitsu camps every year. He is also a prolific creator, as you will discover in the video. He also recommends the author and chess master (which is dope)

James Altucher who talks about ideas as a muscle that needs to be developed and strengthened. Very few people create anything or do anything. This is mostly because they are under the illusion that they have no time or value.

I had a priest (who was a purple belt in jiu-jitsu) visit my studio and tell me that he had no time for jiu-jitsu, and then ask if he could come on the weekends and just train for free. I said no, he would have to pay regardless of how little he could commit to training. A friend of mine, ironically, is also a priest, and he is free of work typically from Wednesday to Saturday morning because he is always outside working on a project...go figure. So, we think we lack time because our distractions beckon us. We have been convinced that we need our television and our social media, but none of those things provide love or warmth or actual human interaction. I am convinced that most comments on any social media post are generated by bots because people never act or speak that way in person, but people assume others are hateful because of said comments.

If you feel your life could be better, or you have voids you want to fill, begin the change by setting a goal. Join a club. Read more books. Invest time in yourself and get to know yourself. Nobody cares if you go social media silent or take a break from social media, as they will just scroll on like you never existed in the first place. When someone dies or leaves the room in real life, people invariably move on quickly, why would the social screen transmitted world be any different? One of my buds (who is a great guy) is an eccentric nut, an absolute whackadoo on his social media platform, and his posts are somewhat funny, but always somewhat shocking. But no one really cares if their feeds are devoid of his musings. No one blinks an eye when he decides to lay off for a few days or goes social media silent, and this goes for all of us. We have sold our souls for likes —a pixel on a screen that resembles a thumb, meme, or a smile emoji.

I did not have to watch the *Social Dilemma*, which was recommended by a student and friend, as I was already in tune with my addiction and on my way out that door. But this is real. Think about the idea of the mouse who has been placed in a maze. If he goes right, he can remain stuck in the maze and receive small food pellets to remain alive (although by meager standards), but if he goes left, he can leave the maze and experience life and all the wonders and possibilities that await him. Also, he can read the signs regarding what each choice will provide for him. People of today are that mouse, and most have chosen to stay in the maze only to be given little food pellets via social media likes and hopes of being internet popular. It's a modern-day middle school for adults.

You want to take control back and have an abundance of free time and energy? Put the phone or television remote down and go outside, breathe some fresh air and then decide what it is you want to do or learn. Do you want to take dance lessons, music lessons, singing lessons? I have met many people who envy my ability to play the drums and guitar. Why? You have everything you need to start playing drums or guitar. Get some chopsticks and bang on some pots and pans to start; that is what I started on. Stop by your local music store and inquire about lessons. Why not attempt to learn? Why not tap into and exercise your right brain? The opportunity is out there, but you will never discover any of it if you remain sequestered in your cage taking happy pills from your social media account like Pavlov's dog. Obviously, all addictions can be distracting, but the modern-day demon that is taking over our lives, our parents lives and our children's lives is the almighty handheld device. It's even gotten to the point where my parents struggle to hold a full-length conversation without gripping their device to stare at it's evil glow. This proves no one is exempt from the charms of distraction, but if you are tuned-in to this realization, and willing to work for it, you can take your life back.

I have zero regrets for being able to control myself around my little pocket pal, as my regrets from the past were because of all the time I used to waste reading about garbage that I cared nothing about. Also, I have greatly reduced my stress-load because I am not inundated with all the negativity and useless memes that are passed through the social pipeline. As if the above information wasn't enough, the blue light, that is cast from your phone, is also a reason many people struggle with sleeping disorders and eye strain impediments. It can restrain the production of melatonin, which is responsible for your sleep & wake cycle. Not receiving enough sunlight during the day can also lead to this problem because your body relies on the use of serotonin (which is gained from sunlight) to help convert to melatonin, and melatonin is necessary in regulating our sleep-wake cycle.

Prior to kicking the habit, I used to spend close to an hour on my phone before attempting to sleep, which again was one of the ways I was losing the war against the addiction. Even when I only sleep a couple hours, because of a busy night on the medic or fire truck, I always feel rested and can function the next day because I leave my phone out of my nighttime routine. If you are so used to the addiction aspect of your device, try purchasing a Kindle or other similar device, and read before bed. This helped me immensely to kick the habit, and now is part of my nightly routine.

Of course, not all time spent in the social media world is wasted or negative. However, like imbibing donuts or ice cream, the key is moderation, and control. If you have control over your addictions, you are winning. In the end, if you want to regain your life and reach your full potential, put the phone and TV remote down and get moving and living —your body and mind will thank you.

# CHAPTER FOURTEEN: PEW PEW

*"You know why there's a second amendment? In case the government fails to follow the first one."*

—RUSH LIMBAUGH

*"Arms are the only true badge of liberty. The possession of arms is the distinction of a free man from a slave."*

—ANDREW FLETCHER

*"Is it a gun problem? Jim Jones killed 919 people with Kool-Aid."*

—LIBERTY ARMS BILLBOARD

There are two things one can do to make men powerless; you can take away their superior intelligence and ability to think critically via creative vision, and you take away their ability to defend themselves. You are reading my book, so naturally I believe intelligence to be important, and as for guns — Yup, I am for them, and I like them. There is nothing quite like the sound of lead plinging against metal. Our forefathers, and the true statesmen of the time knew this, and it is why it is the second amendment. My sons, my wife and I all understand how to safely use and maintain guns. I have never been in the military or a police officer, and my father was a glorified city boy that never hunted, so my experience with guns has come from my own interests and motivation. I believe learning gun safety is a must. My wife and I took a class on gun safety before purchasing a gun. I then spent several hours, at the range, practicing trigger discipline, range safety and target accuracy.

When my sons were around eight and ten, I took them to my buddy's house to shoot. I allowed them both several rounds on the 22. I then however loaded one round, and one only, in the Glock 9mm. I carefully placed the gun in their hands, and I held on too. They fired the gun, and instantly realized the power the gun was capable of. They knew instantly, it was not a toy, and could cause incredible harm. This moment left an indelible mark in their minds. Also, I only gave them one round in case they jerked their body once the round was fired, which of course they did. My boys never once were curious about guns after this, and never displayed the desire to glorify or glamorize guns. Because I safely taught my boys how to handle a gun, firearms were no longer taboo, and the mystique was gone. I did not teach them that guns are scary and menacing, despite what "experts" on the mind control box try to convince us to believe. I also purchased my oldest son a 22 rifle for his birthday, shortly after this experience.

When I was growing up, I would watch action movies, and one of the actions the protagonist would often perform would be to draw their seemingly sharp sword blade over the palm of their own hand. Somehow this never drew blood. Seeing this and wanting to be a warrior like the actors, when I was around six years old, I took my dad's razor blade knife across my hand, and it cut me good; Blood was shooting from my hand like a broken paint sprayer. Again, I was only around six years old, and learned a valuable lesson. Guns are no different. If you allow your kids to play first person shooter games or watch any movie with action, they will be more likely to want to experience the sensation in real life.

I can only imagine what kind of trouble I would have fallen into if I had stumbled upon a gun instead because of my inquisitive nature. I allowed my boys to know, feel and understand the power of firearms, and they understood how dangerous they are based on experience, not fear or curiosity. It saddens me greatly when the fear mongers try to take guns from law abiding citizens because they have been convinced guns are evil. Some of the most well educated, generous, soft spoken and unassuming people I have ever met are staunch gun owners, who conceal carry, and that is great.

Guns are harmless unless placed in a person's hands. I have quite a few guns, and they have never decided they were going to leave their case, exit my gun safe and go on a shooting spree, and I am quite sure this will never happen. The anti-gun agendas are absolutely flawed in their message. Guns do not kill people. People kill people, especially when people are angry and feel dissociated from living in a place where there is doom and gloom on the television morning, noon, and night. In countries where guns are difficult to come by, they use machetes or other objects as a means to maim and harm people, or the bad guys somehow are still able to acquire AR's and AK's. These are also the countries where dictators rule and human trafficking is completely rampant. We need to address the evil that exists in the world, and the over prescribing of drugs like Ritalin, if we want to see less injuries or murder. Instead of demonizing guns, a change in how the media conditions the masses is what is needed. I have read the book *Propaganda by Edward Bernays*, and I understand that fear and negativity equals ratings and action toward an agenda. Also, many authors on the topic of "gun control" have read the book *Don't Think of an Elephant by* Lakoff, and understand the importance of framing and emotion to elicit results —basically the squeaky wheel gets the grease. Instead of convincing us all that the world is a convoluted mess, why not focus on the daily magic and beauty that life provides.

I am grateful everyday that I wake up, as life is a gift and it's over quickly. I am also incredibly grateful that those holding the lines carry guns, so they may effectively do so. No amount of doom and gloom propagated by the media will convince me otherwise. Imagine if every person understood and respected the life ending power of guns, the fear mongering would stop as would the needless deaths. In my line of work, I have worked many gunshot scenes, and tried to save a person the other day that was shot. As the saying goes, bad guys will always find a way to procure guns, so the good guys need them too. No matter how many wounds I have witnessed and will try to heal in my career, I will not change my opinion on gun ownership.

In late 2019 early 2020, our state officials tried to impose an ammo limit and wanted to change the nomenclature of certain laws which would have made it illegal to own a double stack Glock, which is a semi-automatic pistol; it would have been a step in the direction of disarming the citizens of many of their legally procured firearms. In response, many localities in our state, ours included, became "second amendment sanctuaries", Where it was decided no matter what the state officials voted, we were going to be keeping our guns. When our state officials tried to take our guns in January 2020, enough gun owners went to the capital and scared them (not with threats or one ounce of violence, but just by attendance) and the other lawmakers. There were thousands of legal gun owners in attendance, and they made their presence and opinion known. That day, it was proven that if you bring the numbers, you can alter the course of democracy...or at least prevent those in power from attempting to steal it. The end result of this wonderful show of freedom was they did not take our guns.

With so many thousands of gun carrying citizens in attendance, not one bullet was fired, which proved the saying is true, if there was a gun problem in our society, you would know. However, the Governor declared a state of emergency prior to the calm rally, and interestingly, only one person was arrested for wearing a mask in public. —You cannot make this stuff up. We do have a crime problem, but that is for a different time. There are close to 308,000 registered guns in Virginia, and according to efsgv.org, 342 deaths in 2019 were by Homicide —which were most likely illegally owned. So, again, if law abiding citizens were misusing guns, you would know. But such is not the case. As for the peaceful rally at the Capital, once the mission was completed, the peaceful citizens cleaned up after themselves to prove what real men and women, who value their rights, can do when provoked by lawmakers who have forgotten what it's like to reside in the real world. There was no looting, no shooting, no one arrested (except for the law breaker wearing the mask —so nefarious I know) and no trash left on the streets —and mostly everyone was carrying a gun.

Sadly, this example of virtuous patriotism was never celebrated by the media, because the incident rendered their agenda impotent and unsuccessful. They left the fight with their agenda, a limp noodle at best, and their tail between their legs. The agenda also showed how little our "leaders" know or care to know about the people they serve. If you walk into any store, in southern Virginia with a magazine rack, you are always guaranteed to find a gun specific magazine amongst the group, and usually with an emphasis on the AR-15. Just yesterday, I took notice of five different options for firearm specific magazines, at my local grocery store. I guess it could be argued that the people of Northern Virginia believe they run the state —these are the same people perhaps that are trying to ban gas powered leaf blowers because they are too "noisy".

Guns do not have feelings, and do not shoot people. Again, people shoot people. Let us try and help increase the love and vibration amongst humanity but leave guns out of it. You see, if citizens had no guns, they would be helpless to the whims of their leaders or anyone with the mind to impose evil, and this is extremely dangerous. If one finds this knowledge difficult to digest, unfortunately history is replete with power obsessed men with nefarious desires. How about the megalomaniac Adolf Hitler, the man that *Nostradamus* predicted as the second antichrist; though he had him named as Hister, his prediction was eerily accurate. If all the people that had been forced from their homes, collected in a camp like animals, tortured, forced into slave labor and killed, would have been armed with the modern handguns and rifles of their time, the history books would have been written in the blood of the Nazis.

This is how tyranny and slavery are proliferated because one group of people have the monopoly on weaponry over the other, and therefore can perform whatever harm or ill deeds they desire. The Holocaust was real, and it could happen again. So, let us all do the right thing and buy some guns and safely learn to use them, so that the atrocities of the past shall never happen again. Also, it's the second amendment, so our forefathers knew owning guns was an absolute must if you ever really want to consider yourself a true American. If you are adamantly opposed to guns, that is your right, but I suggest you befriend someone with the opposite attitude because if the shit ever hits the fan, and martial law declared, no amount of debating or rationalization will save you from the whims of evil.

# CHAPTER FIFTEEN: STRESS AND ANXIETY

*"To have your head in the sand, you have to be on your knees."*
*"Fear is a vibrational box."*

—DAVID ICKE

*"The most common way people give up their power is
by thinking they don't have any."*

—ALICE WALKER

In an article written by *Peter Wehrwein, titled Astounding increase in anti-depressant use by Americans,* government health statisticians' figure about one in every ten Americans is on antidepressants. I have recently come to realize that I know many people who personally take happy pills, and I must assume from speaking with them that it's the end result of stress and anxiety. I also know a handful of people who are on leave from their occupations for psychological reasons. So many tortured souls on this earth serve this master, and it only seems to be becoming more prevalent.

Interestingly in the engineering world, they have a clear definition and understanding of stress; in that realm, stress can be expressed in any units of force divided by any units of area. In the world of humans however, this malady is ubiquitous and completely misunderstood. Stress is the result of allowing either the negative, fear, or frustration to rule your life, and it is preventable and unnecessary. As human beings, we have a built-in mechanism that alerts us when our thinking or actions are causing the system problems —it's called stress. We are not meant to reside in stress, and copious amounts of it is not normal, despite what most television and radio ads try to convince us. But we are not told this, and sometimes it takes an awakening to see it. Even if you are an atheist, you are not exempt from stress and anxiety. But I really do not know who you turn to when your life goes south. By society's standards, I am an outlier or a "contrarian" as a term utilized often in the book *Zero to One*, because I do not allow stress into my life, and as crazy as this sounds, I have found that makes me supremely different. This is not to say I never feel the pull or pulse of stress, but I make it a habit to never dwell there.

I have owned two businesses, one in which the stereotypical worker is a drug addict or alcoholic, have two children, am married, and work the second most stressful job (firefighter & paramedic) according to the website *Agility Pr* based on a study performed by Career Cast in 2019. But I sleep well at night and am not being bullied by stress. In fact, ninety percent of my time is spent being grateful and smiling. If you are miserable and overrun with stress, I hate to be the one to break it to you, but you have made the choice to allow this to happen to yourself. I had never used the statement faith over fear before 2020, but that would be the message I would go on to proliferate.

Early on, during the 2020 debacle, I told one of my coworkers that I was not afraid of the virus and knew I would not get it. He bet me twenty dollars that we all would (he is little bit of what of we like to call in my household a negative Nancy) —I still have yet to get paid and have also lived the healthiest year of my life despite the media trying to convince even the extremely healthy that they are "asymptomatic". Also, I always knew people's true nature is exposed during times of trouble, and I witnessed many people I thought were pipe hitters lose their wits and display panic during the early phases of the virus. But I never did.

Fear is synonymous with stress, and in Joe Dipspenzas book *Becoming Supernatural,* he mentions how the more you stress, the more chemicals your body will release and then you get caught in a loop of fear and stress. So many people were and remain influenced by fear and therefore allow their chemistry to change into one of constant stress. This seems so obvious to other freethinkers I have talked to, that the more you worry, the more you stress. The more you stress, the weaker you become. Dispenza also mentions a study that was done by Johns Hopkins University that showed a direct correlation between those with a more positive outlook showed a reduction in cardiac events, as in less likely to have a heart attack. A report on the research was published in the *American Journal of Cardiology.* The Study leader Lisa Yanek states, "If you are by nature a cheerful person and look on the bright side of things, you are more likely to be protected from cardiac events." She also states, "A happier temperament has an actual effect on disease, and you may be healthier as a result." This article was written in 2013, so the proof is out there that you must make the choice to live happy —you have to choose the good life if you want to live and sustain a healthy existence.

As for living the last year, I did not breathe through a dirty piece of cloth when I could help it. I wore an N95 mask when responding to medical or fire calls and shopping while at the fire department, as we were getting paid while doing so. I allowed my students to breathe at my studio and did not close off the water fountains. It does not take a scientist to realize breathing and clean water are necessities to a healthy life. Research *Wim Hof,* a man that has proven through actual science that proper breathing techniques unlock our potential to maximum health benefits, if you believe the erroneous statement that breathing fresh air is bad for you. Also, it is the beginning of May 2021 as I edit this, and I have yet to take a Covid test over a year into the madness because I have not needed to. I know more people than I can count that have been tested a multitude of times for the virus, and few that have acquired the Virus are all still living and doing great.

How do you try to convince everyone that they could be virus carrying parasites...especially by the media, by using words like asymptomatic; it is another word for completely healthy, but in 2020 meant you should not be allowed typical freedoms. I also knew how crazy this sounded, that I was completely unafraid of the virus, to most people, as most people have their head in the sand about the law of vibration and attraction. It's not entirely society's fault, as they have been conditioned to buy into whatever the box on the wall tells them to. Also, I had never learned of the law of attraction until I discovered it on my own. The entire situation also did, and still does, feel eerily like the movie *They Live* where all the signs are telling us to obey, as there were many signs and billboards posted throughout the city telling people to wear their masks, wash their hands and keep six feet of distance between other human beings.

Even *Plato,* the famous philosopher, understood this fact when he gifted humanity with his allegory of the cave.

*"Those who are able to see beyond the shadows and lies of their culture will never be understood, let alone believed by the masses."*

—PLATO

He explained how most people would rather stare at the cave wall (the television and news media) and accept the images on the cave over actual reality, and therefore they prefer their chains and binds —and he was alive centuries before Christ walked the earth. This is also akin to Cypher's character in the *Matrix.* After being 'awakened' to what was really going on and realizing the truth for so long, he felt ignorance was bliss, and wanted to return to the false brainwashed reality that most people are thrilled to remain in because it's more comfortable not knowing the truth. Somehow, people alive today still do not understand this. Philosophers have been warning us about this for over two thousand years, yet we remain shackled by false reality and fear.

The news media, where we get the totality of what we are being convinced is our reality, is owned by six corporations, and the talking heads delivering the "facts" are actors reading a script; if you care enough to look beyond the message, you can even see all the computers, equipment, and electronics in the background of the "newsroom". It is a highly funded manufactured "reality".

It is abundantly clear; we have an illusion of choice. The people pulling the strings of our society have discovered it is within our nature to prefer less choices and limit ourselves because most people are not willing to read or do the research required to truly make informed choices. Think about it, Home Depot or Lowes, Coke or Pepsi, Walmart, or Target, iPhone or Droid, Republican or Democrat, Dominos or Papa Johns, Sheets or Wawa, Sam's Club or Costco, Visa or Mastercard...the list goes on. There are other choices beyond this duality in products and politics, but inherent group think, massive inundation from constant symbol (logo) use, advertising and conditioning drive our decisions into a narrow field.

Six corporations (really the big five), own 90% of what we read, listen to, and watch in our society; I cannot help but chuckle and eye roll as I am typing this, as this is madness, but considered absolutely normal and expected by most people who have accepted their cave like reality. With 330 million people living in the United States alone and receiving their "news" from a mere handful of providers, most believe they are receiving truly objective information...hilarious indeed. Next time you listen to an "alternative" radio station, or any station, take note of how many of the same songs they play every day; the insipid song list is indicative of our current choiceless reality, or at least that is the perception.

As for the constant negativity portrayed by the media, this is the reason so many people are poisoned and overcome by stress and anxiety. This morbidly low vibrational state of being told by the media that the world is burning, and you are going to die, is not natural, and leads to high levels of cortisol and adrenaline in our system. We are at the top of the food chain and made in god's likeness. We are loved and cherished by God. We have limitless power, yet we have been kept asleep and conditioned to believe people must be controlled, life is hard and unfair and then we die.

During my thirties? I too bought into the fallacy that you must work hard and struggle, and maybe you will reach the summit someday. I believed loads of suffering was inevitable. Unfortunately, this existence becomes more like the myth and metaphor of Sisyphus and his eternal struggle; whereas if you just decide to quit rolling the boulder and actually move forward by controlling your thoughts, habits and actions, victory is awaiting your arrival. During the 2020 madness, I saw all kinds of hospital and EMS workers posting about staying home and wearing masks. Many of them utilized markers on their vehicles to sell the message that society should stay home for them, because they must work for society. There were also music videos by famous musicians and singers aggrandizing the notion of front-line workers as "heroes". I too was part of the frontlines, and never once felt like this was a fair assertion or request to make of the public. I certainly did not feel like a hero. I felt like the truck drivers and grocery store workers deserve more credit than we did.

I believed I had signed up for this profession, and this was one of those times we had to earn the fact that the public respects us. Most days, we are hanging out at the station, seated on the couch eating food the public brings us, and getting paid to socialize and answer the call when one comes in. So, when the time came to buck up and go to work, I was happy to do so. My wife was never afraid either. We both concluded if I contracted the virus from the job, we would quarantine me in the spare bedroom, and our family would all be okay. I am grateful I was in the first responder world during the pandemonium, so I could see firsthand what was going on behind the scenes. Also, I always believed this label of who is and is not essential is absolute garbage. Here is the truth; as humans, we are all in this together, and the guy who has to sell hamburgers to feed his family and provide a good role model for his children, is as essential as anyone.

Just because we have put a higher social status on doctors, nurses, fire fighters etc. does not mean that these people are more valuable to the world. Everyone has value. It is all perspective. There is no real meaning of value, or rather it is relative to the situation. If you are in the woods and you have no shelter, food, or clothes, and one person knows how to create shelter, one knows how to hunt and one is a doctor, the doctor is the least valuable person in this scenario, and most likely will be told to sit down and stay out of the way while the others build things and catch creatures to eat. I guess they could burn all the doctor's money to keep warm for an hour or two. Do not get me wrong, doctors are great, and we are lucky to have so many in our society. We certainly need them but placing them so high on the status ladder is indicative of a competitive and misguided society. Asking people to close their businesses and stop living their lives out of fear was wrong.

Napoleon Hill made predictions over one hundred years ago with this statement, *"The danger threatening every American citizen which overshadows all others if the growing tendency to stand still, without protest, while one after another of the rights of free enterprise are, by one pretense or another, being removed."* These words rang so true during the 2020 circus. Most people did nothing, while businesses and free enterprise were threatened at every corner. We however stood up and chose to fight. We chose to thrive instead of barely survive, which was what most were content to achieve.

I have seen the truth. Most of our patients we take to the ER are just unhealthy and believe they are sick. Again, daily loads of cortisol and adrenaline from stress mixed with junk food and sugar (because it does not take a genius to realize there is literally sugar in everything) has made our society sick and unhealthy. I say again, there was not one mention of eating healthy or living healthy during the 2020 Circus, just be afraid and wear a mask — there wasn't even mention of wearing a clean mask. I saw many disgusting masks worn by patients during this time too...masks that would make my bulldog sick.

But society has decided who is valuable and who isn't, and we have bought into it. This is a herd mentality. To an innocent child, who has not been beaten down and broken by the pitfalls of society, their dad or mom is the most important provider in their life, and the fact that neither one is a doctor, nurse, firefighter, or police officer does not make their career choice less valuable. Most would agree that teachers should be getting compensated the most for holding responsibility over our children's thinking, but they are paid a pittance for what they are tasked and expected to accomplish. Because the education system is such a government-controlled assimilation system and highly antiquated, It's no surprise teachers' value is deemed so little; however, I will keep my opinion about that from these pages for now. To allow our government to tell us who was and was not essential is testimony to how many of us are asleep. We were being told by the wealthiest, most privileged sector of our country who was permitted to earn and pay their bills and who wasn't...and many people played along.

I even played along for a little while, until I was tired of seeing a calm and empty ER (during the summer of 2020, our ER was slower than pre-Virus times), but hearing the world was supposedly burning.

During our shutdown (we closed our gym from mid-March to June, and we did not charge our patrons while our doors were closed), I generated enough steam and interest to start a vehicle detailing business. This would have been my third business, as an entrepreneur. I did struggle for a moment, with the ethics of owning a gym and the thought of possibly causing harm to people, so I was looking into other options. By May, I had a few jobs lined up, luckily all friends of mine, but decided I had an affinity for cleaning my vehicles and did not want to launch another service business. Basically, this was a failed endeavor. My captain, who also builds websites, had already created a website for me, and I had a stack of business cards. But I was not afraid to close the door on that venture, as failure does not scare or intimidate me. Also, had I never done those things, I would still wonder if I should have tried that venture, so no regrets.

Sadly, I have found that most people are not as resourceful or not willing to take on new ventures and did not take the initiative to create other ways to make a living. Naturally, all this led to an immense level of even more stress in our society...as if stress wasn't enough of a dominant force before. One of the most common reasons we take adults to the hospital is for anxiety, which is the result of stress. This raises the question, remember when people were still considered shy or bashful? I do not remember the last time I have heard these terms in our local lexicon. Or perhaps the word aloof, which typically you only hear this term ascribed to house cats. Instead, they have been replaced with social anxiety. There is even a new medically recognized "syndrome" for daydreaming called *Sluggish Cognitive Tempo* or (SCT) and of course they recommend medication, therapy and/or lifestyle changes, in that order. Thank god I grew up before the Ritalin takeover, or I would have been a case study too.

I technically suffer from social anxiety, though I will bet money anyone who knows me or experiences my energy would not know this. I often still get sweaty palms anytime I am around anyone other than my family or close friends and am extremely nervous before teaching class. But I have spent years mastering and controlling my shyness. You see, the pharmaceutical industry cannot profit from my shyness, but they can and have built an empire around anxiety. I have never taken Prozac or Adderall or needed the help of a physiatrist, even during my college years —Oh yea, I went to college too. If I had a dollar for every patient that has told me that they have anxiety, I would be kicking it on my yacht with *Tom Brady* right now. Not to say, all these people are not suffering from something, but to herd so many into one category is either an obvious stain on the medical system, or just an overt example of herd mentality.

How do we overcome this dilemma? We take responsibility for ourselves. If we do not like our current place in society or life, we can make changes to increase the joy in our lives. The song *Vacation,* by Dirty Heads is a great song, with lyrics and a message that support this statement. It's all about balance. Once you hand over your power to self heal, you almost never get it back. We live in a world where there are more than enough resources for everyone. The US, especially, is abundant and full of opportunities and resources. There are so many people stuck in occupations they hate, all by choice. Next time you go for a drive, unless you live in the sticks, look around. There are literally thousands of opportunities for employment, and most likely in trades of jobs that you are currently involved in.

In this area of Coastal Virginia, there are over fifteen different fire departments within an hour drive of here —all paid, and they are struggling to keep boots on the floor. If you are a medic, which most firefighters are, you can work in the hospital as a tech or on a private ambulance as a transport medic. Because of the Virus, everyone I have talked to that owns a small business is finding it difficult to entice people to come to work —there are literally job opportunities everywhere. If I hated coming to work every day, I would make changes to change this reality. But most people follow what the television and their phones want them to believe. The word stress is broadcast all the time, over the radio, being pushed like it is a normal thing, typically to sell pills or some other agenda. Just about every commercial wants to convince us we have a new disease or someone else is starving in the world. The pharmaceutical industry spends billions of dollars a year on advertising, yet they have not snared everyone.

Quite often, while I am lifting weights and spending time with the iron, and easily adding longevity to my already lofty libido, the radio will broadcast some new medication to help the typical man over thirty-five years of age achieve an erection, because this affliction is considered "normal". They have dubbed this misery "erectile dysfunction".

Perhaps it was when the same talking heads tried to convince the populace that masculinity was toxic, that tried to convince us that dad bods were the way to win over the opposite sex. You know who wants you to believe dad bods are what women want, the beer, fast food, big pharma and junk food industries...you know, the companies that make billions (with wealthy CEOs) from poor life habits. You can absolutely allow yourself to lose touch with health and fitness via the dad bod, and then form a dependence on boner pills. However, if you are not interested in spending your free time visiting your doctor, the solution is literally beckoning you from every corner.

The solution? It's called a gym, and it will absolutely add years to your man parts and help shape yourself, so you are more desirable to the opposite sex, or same sex if that is your jam —no judgement here. Will it be a challenge at first? If you have chosen a life of sedentary activity, absolutely. To paraphrase strength coach Jim Wendler, he says for every day missed is an equal day you must make up. So, if you have not lifted or exercised in four years, do not expect dramatic results unless you are ready to dedicate many months and years to your training. The alternative is to possibly have a dependence on boner pills. I honestly do not understand how so many people choose to spend their free time sitting in a doctor's office or being relegated to a dependence on beta blockers or ace inhibitors. Have you ever been to a dialysis center? I didn't even know they existed prior to being a firefighter —it's an interesting experience.

You basically sit in a chair while your blood is cleaned and recirculated through your body by a machine for hours. Chronic kidney disease is typically the reason people are relegated to this treatment, and what is the main cause of chronic kidney disease? You guessed it, high blood pressure and unmanaged diabetes or a highly neglected dad bod. Or, if you overdosed on over the counter medication like Tylenol, this too could cause kidney failure –and why would anyone do that? Oh right, anxiety and depression.

I am not a doctor, but I have a student that is one, as well as a PA and one of my students is 65 years young and managing his diabetes by being on the jiu-jitsu mats. To avoid the life of polypharmacy, you must avoid the opposite corners, where fast food and junk food call out to you. Also, through the 2020 madness, I never saw a drought on fruits and vegetables. Ironically, the healthy stuff was plentiful whilst the cheap meats and toilet paper were being hoarded. We live in a time like no other in history, where there is so much food and an endless array of healthy choices.

For example, just after World War two, bananas were still considered a rare delicacy and had been rationed for years, yet they are literally falling off the shelves today. If that was not evidence enough of the importance of healthy foods, bananas release the chemicals that stimulate the production of serotonin and dopamine, the same neurotransmitters that are activated by Prozac and Ecstasy...sounds like ambrosia to me. I do not keep a strict diet. We keep chips and chocolate in the house, but I also have learned to consume smaller meals, and enjoy the less than nutritious options on occasion. I just turned forty, and I have more gumption and gusto down below than I did in my twenties. I also never gained 100 pounds and turned into two of me. At most, during the early dad years, I gained about ten pounds more than needed to keep me warm, but always maintained a place in the weight room.

There are literally hundreds of ways to remain or regain your health. You could do Pilates, yoga, Jiu jitsu, CrossFit, barre, golf, lift weights and eat healthier, take walks outside, or go skiing or snowboarding just to fire off a few options. Not surprisingly, the media never mentioned eating healthier, joining a gym, or quitting whatever detrimental addiction was ailing society; in fact, these activities were considered dangerous and mandated to cease and desist while eating yourself to death was perfectly acceptable. For over a year now, we have been told to just stay home, be sedentary, wear a mask and be afraid...very afraid. Most of these so-called life saving devices were worn incorrectly or stored in people's pockets or the glove box of their cars, next to their cell phones and whatever trash is kept in most glove boxes these days.

Litter and waste were also on the rise, as the masks gave people something else to discard with no concern for the environment. You would be lying if you told me, you never saw a surgical mask on the ground during the Virus. Even now, a year into the fear machine of 2020, still no mention of any of the above —interesting. Read the chapters Iron and Jiu-Jitsu if you are seriously interested in the fountain of youth; I have seen so many people's physical and mental transformations that I am truly blessed and grateful to be in the industry and a part of that community.

With the never-ending barrage of advertisements convincing society that they are sick, broken, and unable to flow an adequate supply of blood to their penis, stress levels in the world are at an unprecedented high. For this reason, most people don't stand a chance at finding happiness because their motivation to look has been clouded by false advertising and constant distractions.

We were never meant to sit in cubicles, drive hours every day for work commutes and give up our hobbies and dreams to become part of the system.

My father worked a government job and made lots of money, but he was stressed every day. I have very few memories of seeing him smile or goofing around like I do with my sons. I hold no resentments against my father, as this is what most people do. Also, he was a great role model. When he retired, he realized that his position was filled, and his name forgotten by those that he believed held him in high regard.

This is not something that happens in spite, but it's how it goes. I have had the pleasure of working with some amazing people who have retired during my career, but no matter how lofty the respect was for these individuals, the next day began like any other. And they quickly became nothing more than a memory fading more and more by the day.

It is estimated that the American workforce leaves over a billion paid personal leave days on the table each year, a billion. You do not get that time back, and that is time that you are permitted to take and use how you want to. Instead, so many people choose to believe their company needs them —or their job will suffer if they are absent. Hogwash! It's ego; we want to believe we are this important, but the survey says, we are not. I started and was one half of the reason why my jiu-jitsu studio is growing and thriving. But we are entering year three, and we are ready to build the business so my wife and I can have free time away from the studio. That requires lowering my ego and relying on others to help grow the brand. This also means if something were to happen to me, I would want and expect the studio to survive and quickly thrive through my absence.

If the president of the United States were to suddenly collapse and be unfit for his duties, his position would be filled immediately, and his name relegated to a memory. On a side note, not long ago, prior to the current administration, the internet monopolies censored the president by shutting off his multiple social media accounts; interesting, no? I was painting a year ago for a retired chief from the same fire department I work for. From what others tell me, and he would agree, he took his job very seriously and did not prove to be one the equable leaders and chose to lead with an iron fist. Once he retired, his position was quickly filled and most of his retirement years have been spent making doctor's appointments and fighting various ailments. It would be wise to assume this is from a buildup of years of strict behavior and a stress filled existence.

I do not remember my father or mother ever taking a sick day or many vacation days, when we were growing up. You see, so many people believe they are so important that their jobs could not function without them. They choose to spend their best years, worried and stressed about their jobs. Oftentimes, the things that have been stress worthy were not that important at all. Once you retire, and I mean like the next day, they will move onto the next topic and person to fill your shoes. This is not a bad thing. You should want to help build and mold those around you, so your creation can thrive even when you are gone. Therefore I encouraged my wife to start teaching jiu-jitsu not long after earning her blue belt. If something happened to me, I wanted to be sure she could keep the school going.

I study my protocols and train firefighting scenarios to stay sharp at my craft, but if I make a mistake, I own it and move on. I take plenty of days off and leave my work at work. Bringing your work stress home and tainting your home environment is theft. You are stealing the good energy that should be part of your home life. Energy is real, and you always have the choice to shape your environment based on your energy. Your family, or whoever you live with should not be punished and forced to bear your burden because you allow work to break you. I was a victim to this for quite a few years in my thirties. I would have a rough night on the medic or firetruck, and then had to paint the next day. It was physical labor and arduous, and I did not enjoy the painting anymore. But for a time, I thought I was stuck.

I bought into the idea that life was hard, and you had to man up to make it work. In the beginning you do, but once you gain momentum from planting seeds and making good decisions, you then have choices. But the major fallacy in my thinking was that I thought I had no other options, and I had no definitive plan at the time to change my situation. I also did not use the one thing that makes us humans so powerful, my thoughts. Once I changed my thinking and stopped buying into the false mindset of suffering and lack, my life immediately changed. To some degree, life has its challenges, but there are ways to win the game. That's really what this book is about, how to win the game and retain your manhood all the while. Also, I want to help prevent you from looking back on your deathbed and wonder why did I take everything so seriously —why did I not see all the joys and wonder that life was meant to provide?

It's all there. I promise you; life is good, but you must tune in to see it. In a way stress is a luxury because it implies there are other options, and there are other options. We live in a country of endless opportunity, yet we settle for so little. Do you think people in third world countries (people on our planet that are in a constant state of survival and suffering) have the luxury of suffering from anxiety, and then receiving treatment for it? If they went to the one doctor in the whole village and claimed they were suffering from anxiety, the response would be, "well no shit!"

When we closed our business in March, I did not fear loss of wages or paying our bills, as I believed the creator would provide, and I was right. I also did not give credence or worry that we were technically closed at this point, as this was survival. We had no income from our studio, and neither my wife nor I could get anyone from the unemployment office to answer the phone or emails. It felt as if desperation and destitution was the mindset the system was hoping for us to accept; the problem with that was, my wife and I are doers and thinkers, and thinkers figure things out.

Our painting business had been dormant, as we had chosen to stop painting to focus on our studio, but we had a friend and former customer 'magically' call who needed his deck stained. He wanted two different colors of stain, so it was a well-paying project. We got the job and did a great job. Then another friend and paint store employee's father fortuitously called and needed his deck stained. His deck was huge and needed two coats, so another great paying job. Both of these projects were outdoors and both paid so well, with my fire salary, we were paying our bills and still stacking up an abundance of extra for savings. I believed we would be okay financially, and the creator answered the call with two random well paying projects. I also remained stress free during this time and purchased and new toy and truck.

You could say, oh you just got lucky, or what good timing. Yes perhaps, but I asked the higher power for ways to provide, and they were given. Had I been worried or relegated to fear and stress, like so many others, the higher power would have granted this reality and given me more to worry about; trust me, as that was my mindset in my thirties. Instead, I chose to remain faithful to my journey and believe good things were coming. I attracted the reality I wanted. After reopening our studio in June, and then seeing how quickly the media went from pushing the Virus to pushing civil unrest with protests (this was the summer before an election mind you), I knew then that we would not close our business a second time. We decided not to be part of the political parlor games. They had been pushing this "new normal" prior to any real changes in a way that appeared to have been a planned change all along.

We did not put signs on our door that required mask wearing and compliance handed down by the fear machine. We did not cover our windows in paper to hide what we were doing, as I was too overtly disappointed with how few people were willing to fight against the financially elite who deemed them unessential. At this point, about three months into the virus, I had seen no one with this deadly disease that was threatening to wipe out the entire planet. During the wave that occurred around November, I knew a handful of people that were exposed to the virus, but their symptoms were consistent with a cold. These people were also spending their time in the gym; they were healthy. I even knew a few unhealthy people who had gotten the virus, and they too survived. Also, somehow colds and the flu had just disappeared from the earth, only the Virus remained. I told my students and myself that if I thought we were doing more harm than good, or actually hurting people, we would close our doors.

I also thought, I wonder if the people selling cigarettes would consider closing their doors knowing that it has been proven that what they are peddling causes COPD, lung cancer, exacerbates asthma, and leads to immunodeficiencies which were causing most of the deaths? Nope! In fact, those places keep multiplying. Interesting, no? However, I also believe even with the sentiments above, though this is based on fact, they too have the right to continue and grow their business. If the creator granted us free will, then who are we to deny it?

Because of all of this, I was willing to fight to keep my business open and would gladly stand up to any government entity that would try to impose their will. In the biography *Benjamin Franklin by Walter Isaacson,* there is a well-known quote by Franklin that so vividly supports my opinion, he says "*Those who would give up essential liberty to purchase a little temporary safety deserve neither liberty nor safety.*" Let that sink in; reread it if you have to. So many people chose to follow mandates based on fear and chose to allow the government to control every facet of their liberty. I told my wife that in the worst-case scenario, if we lost everything standing up to tyranny or fascism, I would gladly move somewhere warm and coastal and live amongst the ocean swells. Have you been to San Diego? It's absolutely beautiful. The government there is a little cuckoo, but I would gladly be homeless and in the San Diego sun than oppressed in a cage of mental tyrannical slavery. It also appears these days many have decided to do that, as the homeless numbers in California keep rising. But honestly, I would not be homeless for long, because I understand the secret and I am doer. Instead of being stressed at the possibility of the health department knocking on our door, I had already decided I would gladly ball up and toss in the garbage any paperwork they would possibly levy at us. I did not know it before the virus, but I will always fight tyranny and fascism because I am free and under God's rule.

You see, there were examples across the globe of people standing up to tyranny (one of the earliest was a BJJ gym in California ironically and a couple gyms locally), and if you were willing to tune into this frequency, you would see these government entities were truly powerless in these situations. You did not hear about these brave establishments through the media, because the machine fears that this blatant fearlessness would catch on and possibly cause a rebellion. The idea of lockdowns (which is an overt prison term by the way) is at best draconian and overtly unconstitutional. The government was treating the world like one big prison, and when that was ill received it became like a parent child relationship, where we had curfews and could only consume alcohol during limited hours. Luckily, I do not drink much, and enjoy an abundance of sleep, or I would have had to resist and refuse to comply with the curfews as well.

There is and always will be a force in the world called natural law, and as long as you do no harm to others or oppose your will on others, the universe and God will support you. Why do you think the US, in the beginning years, became a free country (aside from the uprising that kicked off from the Stamp Act of 1765), and was considered one nation under God — our forefathers were learned statesman, and knew a relationship with God was the key ingredient to freedom and love on this planet. In 2020, keeping any business open did no harm to others, and those truly in charge, behind the iron curtain, knew this to be true, otherwise giant entities like Walmart and Home Depot would have been at the helm of the problem.

Fear and poor lifestyle choices were the reason the Virus was considered deadly, among all the other things people like *David Icke and Jim Marrs* talk about in their books. Old age was also considered a reason, but let's face it if you are in your 90s, you had your chance at a good life. Every day thereafter is a blessing, and when I am 90, I certainly would not expect the world to quit living their lives to save me. I would not expect it now at forty. When you realize this, you then have a choice to remain in the prison of your mind or step out into actual reality. Something magical happens when you have this mindset, you fear nothing.

I knew that physically, there would be no one that would come into my business and lay hands on me to get their way —my head coach is a SWAT officer for our city, and an absolute marvel of a man. My hope was if the stuff hit the fan, maybe I would be lucky enough to have him to deal with. I would tell other friends and gym owners to open their eyes and look at reality. The governor is not and will not come to your business and force their will upon you with an AR-15, or even a bat or other club like device. When thousands of law-abiding citizens did so (by descending upon Richmond) in January of 2020, he was too afraid to show his face and address the public before him. I really struggle with this level of cowardice.

When he first told everyone they had to wear masks, early in the Summer, and was asked what would happen legally if not obeyed, he stumbled and skirted the question because he knew his demands were Orwellian in nature and unconstitutional. Also, around the same time, he was seen and photographed with citizens unmasked and responded by saying he did not know they would be taking pictures. It's an illusion of control, but many were too afraid to promote their business or even reopen completely. Had the government encouraged the use of masks, as opposed to mandating them, this would have been the choice for a free and educated society —but it did not shake out this way.

Fear of consequences is why so many people quit and closed their businesses, not the Virus. Viruses have been around forever, and unfortunately people leave this earth because of them. People also die because of vehicle accidents, falls, burns, medical malpractice mistakes, starvation, shootings, poisoning, stabbing, heart disease, diabetes, domestic violence, obesity, animal attacks and on and on. In the 1930s, average vehicle accident deaths were around 36,000 and in 2019, there were 36,120 vehicle accident deaths, but we continue to drive cars without a care in the world.

If the media chose an agenda to ban motor vehicles, which could happen, and bombarded the public with statistics and images of deaths from MVA's, eventually all the media followers would be riding bikes and trying to convince the rest of us that we are evil and selfish. Not long ago, we would see images of people in Asian countries walking around donning surgical masks in public and think how silly or ridiculous that is. China also has limits and government control over their internet and media sources, not unlike all the Facebook, Instagram and YouTube posts that were removed or policed in the US because they did not play well with the narrative of the year. With all the various ways that life could end, why not focus on all the beauty and wonder that this life entails.

You can beat and eliminate stress by focusing your attention and feelings on the good things this world has to offer. Regarding the 2020 circus, through all the nonsense about what not to do, such as shaking hands or sharing an intimate and close encounter with friends or family, there was never any mention about starting over and beginning to live a healthy life. Over thirteen months have gone by since this all began, and imagine if the agenda had been to whip society into shape. Most people would be living healthier and happier lives if the media were recommending this, but this was not the agenda. The only way we can all end up like the abdominous blobs in *Wall-E*, and reliant on our addictions, is by being afraid and believing that the media has our best interest at heart.

Success could be final, and final would entail no dependence on drugs or unhealthy foods to curb our stress and anxiety. There was not one mention of eating organic, or more fruits and vegetables and eliminating GMOs from our diets. The government did not swoop into your local grocery store, and forcefully remove all the ice cream, processed foods and packaged garbage that is barely edible. They did however try to force us all to mask the problem. I had been to countless homes (during the Virus) where a patient was having breathing difficulty, was using supplemental home oxygen, and had admitted to smoking multiple cigarettes that day, yet people like this were the reason for the shut down; they were the helpless citizen class we were endeavoring to save.

I have been to countless nursing homes (the ones with cold block walls, where the halls reek of ammonia and urine), where the residents pictures are on the walls outside their rooms like prisoners, and where the residents appear to be dead inside because of the large amount of medications they are on to keep them docile and controlled; these very residents have obviously been abandoned by their family and society, and will die this way eventually. The nurses in these facilities often have no idea who gave the patient what meds, or when they were last seen normal. These are the very people we were desperately trying to save from the virus. These were the ones that now concerned citizens were in belief that one death is too many. I had seen geriatric fathers and mothers too afraid to hug or be within six feet of their children or grandchildren. All I could think is, if your life has been relegated to such a low depth, what life are you desperately trying to maintain and protect at that point...what life are you fearing for? I believe I would hug my child even if they had the most contagious disease in the world, as I would rather suffer with them, then allow them to suffer and die alone.

This is why so many people went to social media with memes about 2020, and how awful it was, and why so many people succumbed to anxiety and depression. This is also when I realized most people are absolutely afraid to do anything. Most of us have been relegated to posting their opinions on social media, with no motivation to actually do anything about it. I wanted nothing to do with this system. Despite what the media was feeding us, we had a choice. When I wrote my goal card to stay off social media, within four months, I wrote this book. I chose happiness and enlightenment. I met over 40 new and awesome people from June to December (I am writing this sentence just before Christmas) and shared rolls and hugs with every one of them. We had twelve new people sign up for intros (at our jiu-jitsu studio) in the first week of January 2021. We never bought into the agenda about staying away from people, and I realized the power of human interaction and positive energy.

There were a few of our students who chose to hold or cancel their memberships because they lived with family members who had compromised immune systems. This actually makes sense, and these are the people we should be trying to protect. But again, the rest of our population is just unhealthy and therefore have made the informed choice to be sick and basically on the brink of death. We are all in this together and need human interaction. Even if you are an introvert, you are not meant to be alone and part of the machine. Read *Machine Stops by E.M. Forster* and you will see a clear example of the dystopian world that the government was trying to create, and what it would look like to completely abandon society as we know it and succumb to the machine. This type of existence is not natural and clearly is not working for our society. During 2020, I saw that it is okay to purchase fast food, alcohol, cigarettes, junk food, sit at home and do absolutely nothing physical, all while gaining weight and losing touch with reality because they have a pill for that.

Guess which businesses you did not see closing, large corporate owned businesses —the rich get richer, yes. The list of all the local places that died with Covid were all locally owned —because a Virus only attacks business names it does not recognize, but the fast-food giants are safe. Also, with the random six feet apart rule, why were they funneling patrons into the big businesses through one entrance and exit? There was never any mention of creating better eating habits or joining a gym. No mention of quitting whatever vices ail you and spending more time on hygiene. New chemicals that were deemed "safe" were suddenly on the market to cleanse all surfaces of this terrible Virus, with no regard for what ramifications this will have on the health and safety of our future. Nothing was said about the energy and vitamin boost that can be gained by going outside and soaking up some sunshine, and in warm tropical areas like California, going outside was criminalized and discouraged. The aspect of community and fellowship was not encouraged, and nothing was said about the cardiovascular benefit of movement in general.

Even church gatherings were criticized and not permitted to occur during the early months. No matter your beliefs about church, this is the therapy and human interaction many people need to limit their stress and find value in their lives, and therefore is essential.

Instead, we were encouraged to stay in our homes, be around no one and wear masks. It was the biggest game of cooties in the history of the world.

When I turned 40, in November of 2020, I decided I was done with allowing stress to rule my life. In my thirties I had been like most people, hot and cold most days with how I handled stress. I had aged more than I needed to because of it, but through discovery, I had enough. Luckily, I had the iron, jiu-jitsu, lots of good books and a great supportive wife to keep me above the level of stress for so many years. Owning a business and being a first responder during the Virus was not stressful, and I made it a point to try and remain upbeat and help raise the vibration of the universe —it's one of the reasons I decided to write this book. I saw more clearly than ever that we are pushed as a society to be a part of the rat race, a part of the system.

I saw exactly what *Napoleon Hill* warned us about, all those years ago, in the book *Outwitting the Devil.* Fear was used against us and created a level of stress in our society unlike any seen in my lifetime.

Sadly, the history books will probably paint the picture that this was the worst pandemic and so much suffering and setback occurred. Though this is true in some regard, all of the above was a choice, and I know many people personally that did not see it this way or suffer at all. At all the local dealerships from Virginia to Maryland, all jet skis and boats were sold out before mid-summer, so there is undeniable proof that many people were not just purchasing toilet paper. Many chose to continue to live their lives. When we are bombarded with stress, as was the agenda of the media, we are forced to utilize our reptilian brain, and therefore only see the world in black and white. Unfortunately for most people this forced them into a constant state of survival.

This is the reason so many people would not hug their children or do the basic things they would normally do in their everyday lives; they were not thinking like normal educated human beings. If you take the chapter about the trades to heart, you will never be unessential, and therefore will have nothing to fear when the world goes temporarily broken again. Not just during the Virus, but other moments I have witnessed in life could have broken me and drove me to the bottle or some other vice to get my head straight. In the fire service, I had seen my share of shock and awe, from many deaths from fires and code blues to a young child that despite myself and others' best efforts, could not save from an unknown condition that caused cardiac arrest. Considering all this, and in correlation with mainstream thinking, I would be well within my rights to take up drugs or alcohol to keep my shit together, but I chose to win, grow and thrive naturally instead.

The band *Falling in Reverse* put out a song called *Drugs*, and it basically states everyone is on drugs; maybe this was the year the machine was hoping would break us all and relegate us to drug dependence. During 2020, my wife and I made advancements and continued to move forward when most people were frustrated, stressed and too afraid to continue, but again, this was their choice. My sincere hope is that since we seem to be entering the age of enlightenment, as youtuber and pro-law of attraction messenger *Jake Ducey* has remained active, and promoted love and abundance, throughout the entire 2020 episode, that more people will find hope and courage and keep fighting next time the wool is pulled over their eyes. My opinion is there is always good to be gleaned from bad situations, as it shows the devil's desperation. If we are truly approaching the age of enlightenment, the devil will keep trying to scare as many people as possible, but the light workers will continue to multiply to serve God and bring love back to humanity. Remember you have a choice to think positive and continue to grow or succumb to the present agenda, whatever it may be. John Milton wrote, "*The mind within itself can make a heaven of hell, a hell of heaven.*" The great Martin Luther King said, "*A man can't ride your back unless it's bent.*" Choose to remain free and keep your loving vibrations high and watch as the stress begins to fade away my friends. You always have a choice, and the choice is yours.

# CHAPTER SIXTEEN: ORGANIZATION

*"Cleanliness is next to Godliness."*

—17TH CENTURY PROVERB.

Yea right! I am laughing as I am writing this, as I have still not uncovered the mystery of organization. The good news is if you have made it your goal to read a chapter a day, congrats you now have an abundance of free time. As for Organization, If I did not have my wife to help me with this constant quandary, I would most likely be lying naked in a ditch somewhere, very cold, and extremely hungry. I do know enough to get by and stay on task most days, but nothing worth writing about. Thankfully, I have her in my life to help me stay organized. As for organization, perhaps someday I will have enough knowledge to seriously generate this chapter. I may decide to go the officer route soon, so comprehending and mastering organization is in my future. Until then, I recommend you turn the page and spare yourself the embarrassment of being caught reading this fraudulent chapter.

# CHAPTER SEVENTEEN:
# THE ZOMBIE

Being a Firefighter and medic, I find it suitable that I must include at least one good story in this book that may have occurred during my years on the job; so here it is. I must first make the assertion that it is quite impressive indeed what that human body is capable of. You can achieve immeasurable greatness, or the complete and absolute opposite of that. Working as a medic, I have seen both sides of the coin. One call I will never forget included a lady that proved zombies are a tangible possibility. We had been called to a house, in a middle-class neighborhood, for a blood sugar check, and when we arrived, the outside of the home looked like all the others in the neighborhood...a brick one story ranch style house with a decently manicured lawn with no vehicles in the driveway. However, we quickly realized the house belonged to a hoarder. Inside, there was stuff everywhere —newspapers, garbage, clothes, dishes, used toilet paper, dirt, dust, bugs and so much more. The inside of the home was dark (the only light was the natural light from the windows) and all the walls were covered in peeling paint, mold and mildew. The copious amounts of debris were piled about three feet high, near the corners of the rooms and hallway, so you had to either walk directly in the middle or duck your head to avoid colliding with the ceiling. Once we peeked inside the home, we realized we all needed to protect ourselves by wearing our bunker gear and SCBA's (self-contained breathing apparatus), which is the same stuff we wear in fires.

It took us a few minutes to don our gear and locate the patient. As we entered the home, we could hear someone calling us, but we were not sure where the patient was at first. After tracking the voice, we found her —the zombie. She was a woman in her fifties, and she could only raise her head from the neckline up. She did not appear to be able to move her legs or rotate her hips, but she could lift her arms. As we walked in the room, she asked "What is that smell?". Naturally, we did not answer this question. She was naked (this was not a good thing) and did not appear to have moved from her location for, my guess would be, months. She was lying supine on what looked like a mattress. It was difficult to tell, as it was covered with trash, feces, and mold. The room was also very dark. There was a window behind her that was operational. Apparently, a family member had been helping to keep her alive by handing food to her through her window. The window was just close enough that she could reach the provisions. I must assume she did not require much in the way of calories. The trash from her meals lay haphazardly throughout the room. I had only been in the department for just under two years at this time, and I'd never seen anything like this, and have not since.

According to the lady, she had only been laying in that position for a few days. Other than this mental misstep, she displayed normal mentation and was aware of her surroundings. We did not check her vitals in the room because it is extremely difficult to do so in bunker gear. It was precarious just trying to stand in the room, and she appeared well for the moment. It took us a few moments to figure out how we were going to get her out —the idea of taking out a silhouette of the brick veneer behind her was one of the options mentioned. No exaggeration, the typical mattress, box spring and bed frame amount to around two foot of height, and we were standing level with her mattress, but on trash, clothing and who knows what. It was extremely difficult to move around, and we were unsure if we would be able to safely carry her out. Eventually, we settled on utilizing a "mega-mover" to get her out, which is a heavy-duty transfer tarp with high strength handles around the entire perimeter of the device.

As we attempted to pass one end of the mega mover under the patient, we then realized she had been laying in that spot for a long time. She was legitimately fused to the mattress. Surprisingly, considering her epidermis was literally growing into the fibers of the mattress, she did not complain or wince in pain when we attempted to pass the mega mover under her. While doing so, we pulled a set of keys and lanyard out of her back, and while passing the sheet, I felt something warm and milky. As I pulled my glove covered hand from under her, I had red, yellow, and brown fluids on my hand. I suppose I paused too long or looked a bit pale while staring at my hand because one of the senior firefighters at my station tapped me on the shoulder and shook his head and mouthed the words "no". I did my best to accept that I had piss, poo and blood on my gloved hand for the time being and focused on patient care.

Once we broke just about all the skin on her back free from the dirty mattress, we took our time carrying her outside. As we exited her room, we saw bugs scurrying about, all over the place and a large ominous streak of brown, red and yellow all down the mattress. To think a human being made the choice to even be in a room like that was unfathomable, but here we were removing a person who had willingly made that choice. Once we got her outside and into the medic, the hazmat team gave us some trash bags and Tyvek suits.

We all took turns changing out of our bunker gear and station wear in the neighbor's garage. On our crew that day, we had all types and sizes; so naturally, the Tyvek suits did not fit everyone. We had to utilize duct tape on a few firefighters to seal gaps and tears that were created while pulling the suits on. Our bunker gear went into trash bags, and we eventually went to logistics to clean our gear. I do not know what ever happened to the patient but seeing that she had what equated to the worst possible bed sores (they apparently pulled a few more random objects out of her back at the hospital), massive infections, and she had not been ambulatory for some time, we all believed there was a good chance her luck would soon run out. Because of this lady, I can now say I have had an encounter with a zombie, and I hope I never do again. I would not wish this situation on my worst enemy, yet someone chose to live this way. I could not help but wonder what must have happened in this woman's life that inspired her to just give up and lay in a disgusting, dirty room, and never move again. Either way Zombies do exist, and I am thankful this one was docile.

# CHAPTER EIGHTEEN: STAY CALM

*"When things get out of control and everyone around you is screaming and losing their minds, look for the quiet one and stick with him. He's fixing to kick in some doors and sort some shit out."*

**—UNKNOWN**

You can sum up this chapter by the picture of the fire fighter with the great mustache and shit eating grin on his face (I shall refer to him as "mustache man"), but what is the fun in that? It is interesting how one image could epitomize a philosophy so well. Luckily, I have been privileged enough to work with some of the best in the business, and what made them special was their uncanny ability to stay calm under extreme duress. When I talk with people who have never been in the military or a first responder, I often explain we are in the remaining calm business. All too often, I have seen and worked with highly cerebral people who cannot keep their emotions together when a scene goes off the rails. Here lies my strengths.

As a paramedic FTO, I will never claim to be a doctor on wheels and may not be as knowledgeable as some of my cohorts, but I will however get the job done and attempt to look good doing so. We have all seen the shows where people are running and screaming, while trying to provide EMS or surgery in the ER. The problem with this example is, we do not run when responding to EMS situations or on scenes. I have worked for departments, where some of their medics do choose to run and rush, and quickly they get as amped as the scene, and things quickly fall apart. It does not matter what shape you are in, when the tones drop, you are bombarded with a loud alarm and then a quick synopsis of what you are responding to. As a human, you must quickly control your sympathetic nervous system by taking a breath and calmly walking to the scene. Running will cause your pulse and therefore blood pressure to rise, which then begins to cause tunnel vision. If you work in a rural department (where it may take thirty minutes to arrive at your destination), then running to the truck makes sense, but in our city, we are never more than four to five minutes from our location, and about five to ten minutes from the hospital depending on which part of the city you end up in.

Now, I am not saying to take your time and casually promenade to the truck, but a quick walk to the truck is optimal. When we are in travel to what could be a complex call, I do what I call pregaming, and I look through my protocols (which is basically a cookbook for drug dosages and treatment plans) to have the proper doses in the forefront of my brain. This is especially helpful for pediatric calls, as we do not take nearly enough to be proficient, and the doses are completely different from dosages for adults. I responded to a call once where I had to tell a stranger why we do not run. It was for a pediatric (he was a young teenage boy) patient that had been hit in the head with a line drive baseball; he was the pitcher.

When we arrived on scene, he was laying on the mound and unconscious. We quickly loaded our stretcher and walked as quickly as possible toward the patient. There was a field full of concerned players and the bleachers were full of stunned fans. As we approached, there was a man yelling frantically telling us to run and asking why we weren't running —he was jumping up and down, waving his hands and yelling as loud as he could in a fevered panic. This added unnecessary chaos to a scene that was clearly an example of pandemonium. I yelled back, "sir, we have to stay calm. If we run, we get amped up, and if we get amped up, we cannot think, so stop yelling." This caused him to quell his remarks and frenetic actions and allowed us to quickly assess the boy and get him help. During the ride to the hospital, he came to, and his vitals were stabilized. I apologized to his mother for yelling at the man but told her it had to be done so we could remain calm and think. she understood.

You see, what the public forgets is we are not robots. We are not mind-less, heartless cyborgs with no empathy for those we serve. We, as providers, are dealing with the same human emotions as the public, only we are not afforded the luxury of freaking out. Staying calm comes at a price, and the price demands that we take our time, take a breath, and perform as if we are in full control of the situation. Running is a sure-fire way to ensure you lose your composure, and your scene gets away from you. If you think about it, you may save seconds by running, but then you will lose that time and more when you cannot think straight because your breathing, pulse and blood pressure is elevated —then you are no better than the untrained observers around you.

Sure, there will be moments in life when time trumps intelligence — where you just need to quickly arrive, apply some brute force, and retreat from whatever crazy thing is happening. For example, one time my oldest son, who was only around two years old at the time, was running toward a merry go round (I am talking about the old school rusty metal disks with bone crushing handles and hyper-speed capability), and it was full of kids and spinning about as fast as the earth. I had no time to think, so I launched into a full sprint and snagged him mere inches before he met his untimely death. Another example, we used to have this rusty metal fence in our back-yard, and it was necessary at the time because we live on the water. Around the same time, the same son (inquisitive little hyena) took off towards the fence like a frightened gazelle, as the gate was wide open, so I had to run and save him that time too.

It's no different than the story of the mother who was able to lift the car off her child when his life depended on it. This is proof sometimes, there is no time for thinking, and quick decisive action is the only solution. But when situations warrant right or wrong decisions, these are the times to remain calm and use your knowledge by taking command of yourself and the situation.

I was in church one time and an older gentleman fell out and appeared to have agonal respirations. Naturally, a collective panic ensued, and the ambient energy in the room went from calm to full panic in a mere second. I quickly rushed over and a nurse member on scene ripped open the gentleman's shirt and began CPR. I called for the AED and checked his pulse. I also told everyone if they were not a nurse, medic, or doctor, to please get back. Once I realized he had a pulse, I took a breath of relief and went through the motions of assessing his vitals. As I realized that he had a pulse, was breathing and was warm to the touch, I began to talk calmly with his wife about his medical history. The insanity of the scene quickly left the room, and I was able to ascertain that he had most likely had a syncopal episode. What I remember about this event, was I had been about five years into my firefighting career, and I had finally started to give myself credit as one of the good ones. I was not and will never be a doctor on wheels; there are some incredibly talented and intelligent medics out there, who probably grasp the deep knowledge more than I do, but I know what needs to be done and understand how to utilize my resources to get the job done correctly and look good doing it.

Another scene I remember vividly was when we responded to a neighboring city on mutual aid. The call was for a psychiatric emergency. When we arrived, I could tell the firefighters on scene were not well practiced, as they appeared nervous and unsure of how to provide care for the patient; typically, that means they are all standing around and look somewhat confused. We have all been there at some point in our career. We call it "screensaver" mode. The neighboring department was a military base, and they took a small fraction of calls compared to what we took —they would do in a month what we would in twelve hours. On scene, the patient was upset and appeared to be unsure of who she was, where she was and why we were there; she was also obviously angry that she could not figure all this out. After checking all possible reasons for her malady, we gave her something to calm her down. The EMS captain on scene was so impressed with how I handled the scene, he asked if I was a paramedic and wanted to know my name. At the time I was only an intermediate (which was one step down from a Paramedic), but I had worked at one of the busiest stations in the city and had learned the art of remaining calm. This captain ended up generating a great letter of commendation, which looks good in my work history folder to this day.

Not everyone will learn the art of remaining calm, as I have seen my share of officers that cannot keep it together when things go south. But I do not emulate leaders who do this. My loyalties lie with those who make their jobs look effortless, or at least I endeavor to learn from them. As stated earlier, I have worked for some great officers. We were in a fire one time removing wallboard from a wall to look for hidden hot spots, and our captain poked his head through the hole we made and with a subtle smile said, "peek a boo". This was the same officer that no matter how crazy things appeared, he never raised his volume or appeared phased by the situation. He performed with the same calmness no matter how intense the energy around him was.

This is no different than the officer that had fallen through the floor in the collapse, who needed to keep his cool to ensure him and his backseat guy would survive the event. This may be an extreme case, but had the officer lost his cool, not only would he have been harming himself, but also the firefighter that needed him to be calm in that calamitous moment. No matter what life throws at you, learn to never lose your wits and things will never fall apart.

# CHAPTER NINETEEN: MONEY (IT'S NOT WHAT YOU THINK)

*"Money is a terrible master, but an excellent servant."*

—P.T. BARNUM

For those who have been convinced the want for money is an evil or nefarious endeavor, you are not alone. For years I believed this to be true too. Like most Americans, I spent my time focusing on work, and believed someday the money would finally arrive because of my hard work and constant diligence. I also allowed myself to be so "busy" for so many years, I never stopped and really studied anything about this so-called sparse resource called money. But then I realized money is not the problem or the enemy. Our thoughts about money are why we are riddled with guilt and anxiety when we talk about the subject. But let us think about money for what it really is.

Money is a concept, or more specifically, money or the dollar rather is fiat currency which means it is not actually backed by anything tangible like Gold or silver and has no intrinsic or useful value. More recently, with online banking and the speculation that the government wants to create a cashless society because of the new world order, money is nothing more than numbers on a screen. Basically, at any point, the government could change course and decide the dollar is worthless like bottle caps. Ironically, after a major fallout, bottle caps could be the next currency. Though I believe ammo to be more likely. Furthermore, we are going further down the rabbit hole of modern currency with Bitcoin, which is backed only by speculative interest. In essence, money is large scale Company Scrip, which was currency exchanged and controlled by the mining and logging industry. This meant the currency could only be used at locations owned by those companies. This led to dependence on those places and forced loyalty among workers, as their scrip was worthless anywhere else except shops owned by the mining companies.

There is, at some level, value attributed to money only because the governments that accept, print and distribute money deem it so. In a less auspicious light, money could also be considered a form of slavery because fear of not having enough money enslaves the minds, energy and time of many, and most people are stuck in jobs they hate, for the best years of their life, because of the desire to acquire money. Also, as of April 2021, the US has a debt of 28.1 trillion, and 78 percent is held by US citizens; this means, the average American, through their retirement money, owns the national debt. Basically, the government is like an annoying relative that keeps borrowing money, with no intention of ever paying it back, and that same relative demands that they make the rules and tell you what you can and cannot do.

But money is not a bad thing, and despite popular belief, money is prevalent and plentiful. Also, like literally everything in this world, money is energy and because it is energy, you can manifest it. According to Factmonster.com, the Bureau of Engraving and Printing produces 38 million notes a day with a face value of 541 million dollars; so, it is actually quite obscure indeed how many people struggle to manifest this omnipresent substance called money, and according to Wattles in *The Science of Getting Rich*, being poor in essence is living in wretchedness (assuming we are in that position because of laziness or sloth) because as a species that has been gifted with ability to think and use limitless imagination, none should find acquiring riches so difficult. An amazing quote by Steve Bow, that also dips into this concept is *"God's gift to you is more talent and ability than you could possibly use in a lifetime. Your gift to god is to develop as much of that talent and ability you can in this lifetime."*

Does it make any sense, that if we focus and work at our talents, that God would not provide the financial means necessary to do so? The problem is when we only focus on money, we lose sight of ourselves. Ultimately, living in squalor, like living in abundance is a choice, as is believing in the paucity of money. It takes a focused mind and heart to rise and achieve wealth, especially when we are being constantly shock tested by the government when prices spike on goods that are deemed "essential", such as beef and petroleum products. However, luckily for all of us, there have been authors and thinkers willing to share this knowledge with humanity. Also, if you want to have lots of money to give and donate to whatever cause appeals to you, you have to possess the money to give; basically, you cannot give unless your own cup is overflowing.

*"The more of life's treasures you keep to yourself, the less you have."*

—WILLIAM DANFORTH

For most people I have talked to, they do not understand the true nature of money, but within just three years of studying the nature of money and how to attract it, we personally have gone from having credit card debt of around 20,000 (we started a new business and I quit my job) and temporarily needing our boys to receive discounted school lunches, to having no credit card debt and earning more than we ever have in combined yearly income, as well as boosting our savings back to lofty levels. Depending on which school you follow, most agree starting at ten percent save ratio to be a good amount to save; I agree this is a good start. Also, we are turning down the opportunity to make extra money by painting houses or working overtime at the fire department. Which proves you can get to the point where money is literally flying at you. How is this possible? Our thoughts and attitudes about money changed —that is what happened. We have a mindset of abundance. The concept of lack is an illusion. Many people are living in a mental state of poverty, and it's called the lower and soon to be middle class.

For many, there is no motivation or belief of possibility to climb beyond the confines of the middle class. You have talking heads on television, whose mission is to keep everyone in a constant state of turmoil, working tirelessly to convince us that we need government handouts, and that money is a scarcity (As I write this, society is due to receive their next installment of "stimulus money", and I had no idea; a student told me this was happening). Yet, wealth exists everywhere in this country, and has existed for many generations. Why? What is the nature of this dichotomy? Most people are gleefully distracted by their celebrities, politics, and the rat race they have been convinced they are a part of.

Most people see the world from fear or the negative. With there being a newly appointed president, naturally gas prices are soaring, to test the public response, and most people are complaining about it. We, on the other hand, have the mindset that the universe will provide more money to offset the increase, and I am thinking this with utmost certainty as I fill my brand-new jet ski (that was paid for in cash) with superior grade fuel. Most people have been convinced they have to hoard and protect money, like it is this precious and sparse resource; when in reality, money is just pieces of paper or more commonly, numbers on a computer screen. I too used to fall victim to this trap because surprisingly, twenty years of school taught me nothing about how to attract money, but once I began studying authors like Napoleon Hill, Wallace Wattles and Bob Proctor to name a few, they were telling me something completely different...and I paid attention.

If you focus your thoughts, beliefs, and energy on acquiring wealth, you can have it. Make the decision to live and be wealthy, and your wildest dreams can come true. I have literally manifested everything I have held in my mind. Yes, it seems like I am just gathering stuff, but what I am doing is having and enjoying experiences. This past year, most people allowed the puppet masters of the world to control their minds and lives, and many people have paid the ultimate price because of it. Sadly, if anyone would read *Outwitting the Devil,* and heed the words in that book, they could have prevented their phobias from imprisoning them. In that book Hill vividly points to two choices we can make, either faith or fear. Most people chose fear.

Listen to most people when they talk. They say things like, "I cannot take that risk, or what if this or that happens", and most of the time, they are unhappy with their current situation, but too comfortable and afraid to risk change. We chose to take every step and action on faith. When I noticed my youngest son was being affected by the shutdown, we purchased a bulldog to lighten his heart and mind. It worked. When I realized my oldest son was also beginning to lose his balance in life, we purchased a jet ski, so he could enjoy our property to its fullest; this too worked and allowed him to have a wonderful summer. My wife always wanted a Tundra, so we bought a Tundra, all in the last year...while our gym was not operational.

The shutdown did the opposite to me; it empowered me. I realized how afraid most people were, and how controlled most people were. I chose to focus on wealth, happiness, and growth, and that is exactly what became our reality. We took risks with our money and believed in the process. We believed we deserved a great life. We stopped worrying about money. For us, it was that simple. Obviously, this takes a tremendous amount of effort to reverse engineer and restructure our thinking and conditioned beliefs about money, but we are proof it's possible. While many people say they cannot afford simple things like a membership to our jiu-jitsu studio —which is 99 a month for unlimited access, for firefighters and police officers—we were willing to pay 300 a month for my son to attend a sport specific gym (which is also owned by a firefighter) to attend two days a week, and the money came. We stopped basing our purchasing habits on price. Money became a way to experience this beautiful world and life, and we realized money needs to be circulated. Fear of spending money and propensity to hoard it only brings this reality back to you. That which you resist persists.

In the times of the cave dwellers, before Television, Cellphones, BMW's or money itself, fire, shelter and food were what equated to wealth (look no further than Maslow's hierarchy of needs to prove this theory), and to those that held thoughts of those things in their hearts and minds, they were able to acquire said items. God is love and knows no limits to what is possible. Everything you see before you today, the couch, television, carpet, dish washer, computers (all of technology) ...everything, has existed since day one. These things were not discovered until recently, but the possibilities have always existed. The potential for these things to exist has always been here. It is not as if an alien vessel decided to enlighten us by dropping a crate of raw materials and instructions to get the ball rolling on said discoveries. What happened was once all of the necessities were covered and deemed plentiful, man decided and believed he could have more, and God obliged.

In *the Science of Getting Rich by Wattles,* he mentions how formless substance and thinking substance work to create things because of our thoughts and our ability to visualize and feel as if we will have what we want and need with certainty. He utilizes the example of desiring a sewing machine, or anything that will add pleasure and ease to your life, and he states that the father is pleased to give man everything his heart desires. Once I read this book, I realized I misunderstood wealth, and understood we are entitled to the kingdom; it is our birthright, but we have to believe we can have it. With free will, we can choose to live under a bridge, or live in a castle; the only real difference between these two realities are the thoughts that took us there and actions that follow.

During many conversations with friends, especially those of staunch Christian faith, they have a negative association with money, almost like they are ashamed when they speak about having or earning it. Does this sound like something God would want? Think about it in this example. Fire and food were the money equivalent or prized commodity and currency of the caveman's generation. Do you really believe God was thinking, okay you can have some fire, but not too much? I do not want greed to overtake you. No, I believe God is benevolent and was taking delight in the fact that his loved creation was finding warmth and happiness, and once these things became plentiful and easy to come by, more and more opportunities, discoveries and luxuries began to manifest for society to enjoy. So, it stands to reason that today's wants and needs should be met with abundance also.

As aforementioned, Wattles speaks about money (or anything positive thing you want to possess in life) and how God does not want us to feel bad or harbor negative feelings about money. He believes it is our divine right to be rich and enjoy all this life has to offer. Also, God wants to experience all the splendor that life has to offer through his greatest creation. Once I began to implement this type of thinking in my own life, things began to change. When I began to purchase big ticket items or services, during the 2020 Circus and shutdown, I decided there would be no buyer's remorse. We made the decision to purchase what we wanted as an experiment to prove that despite the mass hysteria, humans could still live an amazing life. Money has been plentiful and easy to come by since. Just yesterday, my wife and I decided to make reservations at a nice restaurant, so we went shopping beforehand. I purchased a suit, and she purchased some nice shoes. In totality, after our retail purchases, dinner, drinks and tip, our bill this day was just over five hundred dollars. Money well spent because we deserve it.

Years prior, I would have been nervous and remorseful for spending this amount of money on what I would have considered unnecessary spending, but this is not how it is supposed to be. Those thoughts stem from fear and lack of control, and that have been conditioned by the greed and avarice nature of our thoughts. I no longer experience money as something I have to horde and fear. I have read about other authors who, during their journey to wealthy living, purchased suits and dined in opulent environments to be inspired and influenced by the wealthy class.

In the book, *The Seven Decisions* by *Andy Andrews,* he shares an example of billionaire *Aristotle Onassis's* take on gaining wealth, and he says he would start by being a servant to others; This behavior would ultimately place him in the company of wise and wealthy men. He also mentions that during his early years, he would live frugally but save up enough money to eat in expensive restaurants. He would spend large amounts of money to be in those environments with the goal of forming connections and associations with people of wealth and power. He also relates his actions to the notion of kindness (remember the first actual chapter of this book) by saying in those environments, he would hold a chair or door for a stranger, and eventually he would run into those people and receive help, to advance in life, because of his kindness.

My father used to say success breeds success, or you are the company you keep. There are literally trillions of pieces of paper being circulated in the world in the form of money, and endless ones and zeros on your bank account via a computer or cellphone screen. Money is meant to serve you, and if you call out to it, it will listen. All too often, people believe they cannot afford something because of the price tag. We completely understand this thinking because this is unequivocally true; if you believe you cannot afford it, you can't. You get exactly what you believe you should get, and nothing more. Once I stopped thinking this way, everything changed.

The last three years of our lives, since discovering the secret about the law of attraction, have been amazing. In the last three weeks, I have turned away customers from my previous business, with work that would have probably amounted to over ten thousand in profits. But I do not want to labor and lower my vibrations any longer to earn money, as the work is no longer enjoyable to me. Once my wife and I decided we no longer enjoyed painting homes, we decided to quit. We took a chance on doing the things we love, and it paid off. We enjoy the work we do now, and within three years of trusting God and the process, everything has been amazing.

I look at money as a ticket or vehicle to an amazing life, and it needs to be circulated. We pay a gym membership, to a fitness center, and rarely go because we have equipment at home. I am supporting a small business by doing so and proving that money needs to be released to be gained. When I feel like going to lift at the gym, I can go. The universe will allow an adequate intake for this purchase because I am giving back and allowing others to enjoy the abundance in the world. You see, when you spend money freely, and purchase something that has value to you, you are thinking about others and not just yourself, especially with a small business.

Money will arrive in your life when you believe it should be there. Think about all those people that complain that they lack money but spend loads of it on their vices. Often these are the people that dip tobacco, or smoke cigarettes or spend three dollars on an energy drink or designer coffees, and drink multiple drinks a day. If you do the math on that and say an average of six dollars a day are spent on said vices, that is a total of 180 a month on stuff that adds little value to your life...or does it. I also know people who spend hours clipping coupons and scouring the sales paper looking for deals.

They say time is money, but time is intensely more valuable than money. In our three-dimensional Newtonian world of space and time, where space is unlimited and time is finite, we do not have time to waste, but people waste lots of it trying to save a few pennies on their favorite condiments. As for people's vices, it's all perspective right. Maybe it adds immense value to your life. But the point is, they have the money for that stuff.

What it equates to is we are frightened by big numbers, but most people are completely okay with squandering the same amount each month little bits at a time. Therefore, because of low cost, fast food is popular. I hear it all the time, that it is cheaper to eat fast food instead of eating clean, yet frozen vegetables are cheap; and there is always meat on sale at the grocery store. You must ask what is your health worth? In 2016, my wife and I purchased sleep number beds for us and our two sons, and it was a game changer. The beds were an expensive purchase, you could buy a mid-level sedan for the same price, but well worth it. I was bringing in a fire firefighters' salary and owned a small painting business at the time but was literally sleeping like a king. Why? Because I believed I could and was willing to spend the money needed to do so. My wife went from waking up every morning in pain and hunched over for several minutes to feeling no pain and well rested.

The meat and potatoes of this chapter is it's all in your head —your feelings about money are what make it good or evil. If you acquire money and feel you are better than everyone else and you do not want others to have any, this is a non-utilitarian thought process and a sign of avarice. But, if you have money, and you enjoy what money can purchase and are willing to offer a meal or the money to buy a meal to a hungry stranger, then you understand the true value and positive aspects of money. I try to always keep an unused skateboard deck in the car to give away when I see someone on a skateboard. Yesterday, while driving with my wife, we saw a young man sitting on his board. We stopped and asked him to do a kickflip. He tried many times but could not quite land it. He appeared frustrated at himself for not landing the trick, but I told him he did a good job and handed him the deck. He was not expecting this, but happily gave me a fist bump and said thank you as we drove away. I have already purchased another skateboard deck in wait for the next chance to give one away.

The same evening, we gave away the board, we then went to have an early dinner at one of our favorite local restaurants. We had a gift card for fifty dollars, to this restaurant, and our meal was fifty and some change. We gave the waiter a gift card, and exact change, and a one-hundred-dollar tip. We have decided since my wife landed her great government job, to donate 100 (yes, this tip scenario is a little different, but not a bad start) a month to spread love to a human we do not know. Recently, we also had a food truck at one of our Jiu-Jitsu events, and we tipped the owner 100 because of his great service. You have to give to get.

Last weekend, we went out with over thirty friends to a meal and bourbon night. One of our students, who also understands the energy of money, paid for the event to be private for five hours. He declared multiple times that he did not want any money, but asked that everyone tip the wait staff well, since he bankrolled the event. At the end of the night, after drinking around five bourbons (between my wife and I) and enjoying hamburgers, we tipped the waitress $100 and gave $100 to our friend. We also shared an Uber with a friend on the way to the event. When I asked what we owed, he said 25 bucks. I was only carrying twenties, so I gave him 40 and told him to keep the rest.

Also, prior to the event, I purchased a new suit jacket, as I wanted to go out in style. Just three years prior, I would have not been willing to be so generous with our money, and three years prior, money would have and was much more difficult to manifest because I believed in its scarcity. I share the above with you not out of hubris, but to provide real life examples of how money flows when you believe in the power of your thinking and deliberate actions. With the over thirty books I have read about the law of attraction, they all agree you have to have the mindset of wealth if you are ever going to acquire it. Read *Think and Grow Rich*, and *Science of getting rich*, or any work by Bob Proctor if you need more convincing. This chapter about money is a meager paraphrasing of those authors, but my hope is to inspire you to do your own research.

Wealth is an incredible concept, especially if achieving it will allow you your best life and augment your willingness to help others. Just yesterday, I was picking up my sons from a trip to their grandparents' house. We met at a fast-food restaurant. The only thing I will consume from a fast-food stop is sweet tea; for me eating overt Frankenfood is a slippery slope. While waiting in line, I overheard the cashier asking a coworker for a few bucks, as she needed it for something. She then mentioned she would pay her back with a check if she had to. Once I was done paying for my drink, I left the remaining cash I had on hand (it was six dollars) on the counter and told her to have a great day. I felt if I really overheard that she was in need of a couple bucks, then I was meant to hear it because I was willing to help. If I had more cash available at the time, I would have given it to her.

Think about why so many people in America make roughly the same amount and have many of the same problems, because their thinking got them there, and because they see it all around them. Relentless positive thinking takes work, and it takes faith. According to a study in 2017 by the Federal Reserve, and mentioned in an article by the *Washington Post,* one percent of the population control about forty percent of the wealth. What are they doing differently than the rest of us? They think differently, and they have been in environments where those people think differently. If you want to be rich and feel rich, you must think rich. The wealthy are humans just like the rest of us. They require food for nourishment and rest to recharge. They utilize the restroom and require clean underwear like anyone else. Donald Trump is not special, but he did make good financial decisions and bet on himself —he thought and acclimated to riches.

Do not allow parsimonious thoughts to overtake you but know that you can be and have anything you want in this life. Why do you think when people tithe, they do not want for money? One, they are offering their money to a noble cause and for lofty reasons, and two because they believe it to be true —the have desire backed by unshakeable faith as spoken about in *Think and Grow Rich.* Money is nothing more than a concept, and the thought of it really being yours is undeniably false. At best, we are borrowing money while here on this planet. When you die, I am not quite sure where your soul will go, but I know with 100 percent certainty your money will stay here. If you want to forgo living the good life and deny yourself the pleasures of this wonderful universe, you have that right. But you also have a right to experience all the beauty and splendor this wonderful planet has to offer, and if you can imagine having it, and believe it can be yours —whatever it is that will make you happy— then you will have the money for it. Bob Proctor says, *"if you can hold it in your head, you can hold it in your hand."* You must be willing to believe anything can be yours and act when the time feels right.

# CHAPTER TWENTY: LOVE

*"There is only one happiness in this life, to love and be loved."*

—GEORGE SAND

We began this journey together with kindness, so it should be fitting we end it with love. Once you have been bathed in God's great love, there is no going back. I cannot say it will always be bright blue skies and warm fuzzy feelings, though I have taken notice of how beautiful the sky is of late… every morning. It is quite beautiful indeed. There will be pitfalls and snares along the way, but that is the devil and the dark energy of the universe trying to wreak havoc on your journey. Accept it. Understand it and keep moving forward. The bruises and black eyes life will throw at you will heal, as everything will with time. Do not be afraid to share your love. You can certainly provide to others in subtle ways but keep moving forward and keep sharing. Love is energy and perceived wavelength. To understand love, we should first try to understand some things about the heart.

The heart is an amazing part of the human system, it beats because of what is called automaticity, which means it does not require the brain or spinal cord in order to function…it can literally beat without the use of the body. Like most systems in the body, the heart does have an inherent set of characteristics; it has an inherent beat or pulse range (which differ depending on age), and when that range is hindered or challenged because of congenital reasons, hypertrophy, or bad living habits, it resorts to other areas within itself to pick up the slack. Also, the heart can form what is called anastomosis, which is where it generates other ways to circulate blood when the arteries within itself become clogged or stiffened. Therefore, sometimes runners, the ones who have always been supremely healthy, often succumb to heart attacks because relentless high beta frequency stress (as opposed to hormetic stress) from cortisol and adrenaline, released during training, is detrimental in large doses over long periods of time. And essentially, their hearts have never had the chance or needed to create other ways to perfuse itself because it is healthy. I once had to synchronize cardiovert (which is where you deliver a controlled shock) a runner that was in severe SVT (Supraventricular Tachycardia or racing heart) because of this very reason. When we arrived by his side, he was diaphoretic and unconscious, guppy breathing and his heart was beating 280 beats per minute, which is more than twice what is normal. Once he was coherent, after riding the lightning from 100 joules of direct energy to the ticker, he confirmed he was healthy and had no previous medical problems.

I will now provide some amazing facts about the heart provided by the *Institute of HeartMath*. The heart provides the body's most powerful electromagnetic field. Clearly, this supports why love is the most powerful human emotion and the prize for life. The brain obeys the heart. More nerves go from the heart to the brain, than the other way which means more information is passed to the brain from the heart, than the other way around. In fetal development, the heart is formed and starts beating before the brain is developed. This serves as proof of why the brain is for thinking and the heart for feeling, knowing and intuition. According to the institute, when the heart, the brain and central nervous system are in harmony, the person moves to a higher level of awareness. This is absolutely amazing. Whenever you come from the heart, the experience is about love and harmony. The heart does not try to destroy or seek anything negative or create suffering. This is love, and we need to share it.

A good example, of sharing love, is when you show up to work as a firefighter or whatever job you are doing, and the off going shift cannot leave until they have coverage. No matter what time the boots from the other shift show up to work, you should arrive at least a half an hour before the shift. That way if a late call comes in, you can take it, and they can end their shift on time. I see so many people change this about their morning routine in retaliation to the other shift's late arrival time. By focusing on the good habits of your morning routine and basing your arrival time around being there for others, you are choosing love, and therefore spreading light. Also, though it seems small, you are giving to others by sharing your most valuable commodity, time. This example goes for anything that may cause spite to rise in your heart. If a family member does not call you enough (or you feel this to be true), do not return the favor out of annoyance. Instead call them and attempt to open the line of communication instead of adding to its absence.

Another way you can spread love is by applauding other people's accomplishments. We are all guilty of being slightly jealous when someone else accomplishes something great, but with practice we can eliminate this habit and show love and appreciation for others. Promotion is a big one. I hear all too often that so and so was promoted over me. Or so and so got promoted, so now I must because I am smarter than him or better than him. Instead, feel good about the fact that someone you know has accomplished something wonderful. You can choose to feel good knowing the opportunity is out there for promotion, and instead of causing friction and resistance, you could reach out to those who have succeeded to learn from them. We forget that sending out this kind of energy is amplifying the love in the world, and if we can feel good for others, we add to our own well-being too.

We are all connected. Some call it the collective consciousness, the unified field, superconscious mind, or infinite intelligence, but it is real. In the documentary, *I am not your Guru*, Starring *Tony Robbins*, he mentions the importance of infinite intelligence, and how it allows him to help others. Nicola Tesla understood this and had planned to change the world by demonstrating that with enough thought and energy, from enough people, you could power the world through free electrical energy without wires via his *Tower of Power.* *The author* Joe Dispenza says basically we are not simple beings living linear lives but dimensional beings indeed. This truth is displayed in the movie *ELF*, where enough people centered and focused their love and energy, which allowed Santa's sleigh to operate. To the untrained eye and distracted mind, this seems like pure fantasy, but the highest powers in the world know some form of this to be true. The negative powers try to keep us distracted and divided by endless wars, bad news and constant disasters to keep our vibrations low, which feeds the evil and keeps most of the population living in fear. But we must endeavor to keep our vibrations high by spreading and sharing love, and this takes conscious effort and awareness on our part.

Without love, this planet would fall apart, and we would all become prisoners to our own selfish desires. Because we are all part of the aggregate, the more love and unity we can generate as a species, the better for mankind; Speaker Mark Passio does an amazing job discussing this theory through his many lectures. Please look him up for more depth. Imagine a world where third world countries exist, where there is not enough food, shelter, and general provisions to go around —oh wait, that is something that exists, and we live in that world. So, it is not unimaginable to believe the entire planet could be shrouded in this much madness and darkness. Luckily, many countries live by Divine or natural law and utilize love to drive and motivate their lives. Love in relationships is important too, one thought I try to keep in the forefront of my mind is the image of my wedding day.

All too often people look elated and exceptionally happy in their wedding pictures, but over time they allow life to beat the joy out of them, only to fall victim to stress and disinterest. I however choose love and will never fall victim to the doldrums of life and allow it to generate rust in my marriage. Another great example of the power of love was in the movie *The Grinch.* Just after the Grinch stole Christmas from the Who's, he expected to see gnashing of teeth and great hardship amongst the community because he believed they only cared about what was under their trees. Instead, he saw a society, hand in hand, singing and spreading love together. Again, though this appears as fiction, the concept of community and love holds true.

Because of powerful images of communities coming together to spread love, I never bought into the thought of the 2020 madness because when you see the immense love and joy that is inherent in the world, sickness begins to disappear and only love remains. I saw this truism firsthand from the great people at our jiu-jitsu studio, and in the jiu-jitsu community in general. This is also akin to projects of larger proportions mentioned in Joe Dispenza's book, *Becoming Supernatural,* where he references Project Coherence, which were meditations that included thousands of people with the goal of raising the frequency of the planet. He provided data of how they were able to lower crime and vehicle accidents among other negative events. He also backs his findings with peer reviewed scientific studies. This is tangible, quantifiable proof that love is an energy force, and amazing things happen when we use it.

As for our jiu-jitsu community, they were all healthy, happy and full of light because they had that one place, they could go to feel normal, and be around like-minded people. After every class we circle up and finish with a bro hug. The first person in line, whoever is teaching that day, begins to walk around the circle, starting with the last person. We quickly make eye contact, smile, handshake and hug, and every person does this. It is an amazing way to share love and positive energy.

Forgiveness is love incarnated as well. I have had my share of negative moments but try not to hold on tightly (or at all really) to these moments. Forgiving does not mean I have to spend my free time with such people, but it is an unspoken agreement that we will not always agree on things; therefore, I won't allow bad memories to shape my current thinking. Choosing to be magnanimous is choosing to proliferate love.

Sharing the joys of love is also important. On Christmas day this year, we gave a card with a positive handwritten note (thanking them for working and being valued on Christmas) and a one-hundred-dollar bill to a random stranger. We took our sons to a popular convenience store to get coffee, and my oldest bought a piece of pizza. The lady behind the counter seemed sweet, so we chose her as the recipient. After I paid for the goodies, I said this is for you and handed her the card. We promptly left the store and never saw the lady again. My wife and I both were overwhelmed with love, as we just wanted to give the message of gratitude that someone was working on Christmas, and their efforts were not in vain and did not go unnoticed. We then decided to purchase some sandwiches from another popular pit-stop location and distribute those with water to random people with cardboard signs on the street. It was a display of random kindness for others, and a message I wanted my sons to understand. I have always told them their grades in school are secondary to how they treat other people and share their love with others. We have given away so much money to the homeless, I have lost count.

During the 2020 madness, instead of giving and showing love, most people were convinced to go nowhere near other people and wear a mask everywhere they went. There is something dehumanizing about humans wearing muzzles (I say this because my wife is deaf in one ear and it literally sounds like the person is muzzled to her when they speak) and not being able to share one of the most important things that make them human, their smile. This is not natural. Social distancing was a way to keep people from sharing love. The heart's magnetic field is the strongest magnetic field in the body, envelopes every cell of the body and extends out all directions from the body for several feet. Based on multiple studies, about three feet is the distance of the heart's field, so if there is another person involved, six foot would be the combined distance of this energy field. Seems quite ironic that this was the distance we were expected to keep away from one another during the Virus.

Not only were we told and expected to keep this distance with strangers, but also loved ones. It's no wonder everyone was convinced 2020 was the worst year ever. I would hug my child no matter what the cost to my health. As humans, we can literally feel each other's energy, as we are reading the world via frequency waves and vibrations. It's no surprise that because of the random six-foot distance rule and mask wearing that most people looked like zombies and appeared exhausted from stress. We are not meant to be this way. We are loving beings created out of love, and therefore need love to thrive. If we were just meant to go to work, pay our taxes and then go home to repeat this loop on a weekly cycle, we would have all been born honeybees. There is actually a scene in the children's movie *Bee Movie*, where the company told the main character that they would try to work him to death, so they are even trying to convince our children this is normal. As a species, we are meant for more; we are meant for love. What separates us from other creatures is the capacity to choose and spread love through our own endeavors and creations, and this is the gift to humanity. Choose to give when you can and be present when you can. Love is our most precious commodity. Let us never waste it. Love is a choice. Please choose to use it and share your love with the world.

# CHAPTER TWENTY-ONE: THE END

I sincerely hope you enjoyed my work, and never stop learning about your-self. Please take all the negatives within these pages, acknowledge, and accept them for what they are, and then move on. The onus is on us to find balance in our lives, hopefully with a heavy emphasis on the positives. The key is also to never dwell on the realizations and awakenings that occur in our lives, but to use them to improve ourselves a little bit each day. If you can hold an image of your goals, desires and dreams and remain steadfast in the pursuit of their acquisition, your life will be a dream; therefore, you will have no deathbed regrets. One of my most prized possessions is a voicemail from my son, who was around four at the time (He just turned 13) of the recording. He called to tell me he earned a bronze medal, in a wrestling tournament, and that he loved me. I almost generate tears every time I listen to it. The sound of the younger him melts my heart.

The voicemail message is a constant reminder to stop and enjoy this life, and to never allow stress or fear to steal one moment of time that God has so lovingly given me because it is fleeting. You and the people around you suffer when you choose stress or fear, over faith and love. There is an endless world of knowledge and opportunity out there, and I urge you to go out and try something new and learn something new. Everyday is a gift, and your past does not define you. So, no matter how many mistakes you have made in your past, keep moving forward.

One of my favorite quotes in existence is from an amazing and accomplished human being that left this world too soon. *Chadwick Boseman said, "When I stand before God at the end of my life, I would hope that I would not have a single bit of talent left, and could say, I used everything you gave me."* He had it figured out. We are not meant to sit idly and watch the world happen around us. People who think their adult years are meant to be working and chasing the cheese at the end of the maze have forgotten the most important aspect of the search, to stop and enjoy the beauty that occurs every day. This conundrum is akin to the cliche, "stop and smell the roses." *Alan Watts* understood this, as he offers some of the deepest quotes about infinite possibility and wonder. Whatever it is that interests you, no matter how challenging or far-fetched it may seem, go out and do it. *Shia Labeouf* certainly understands this with his emphatic video about "just doing it" and acting, as does the company Nike. Sure, they were mostly just trying to encourage the masses to purchase shoes or acquire a fan base, which clearly worked, but they were also playing into the inner spirit that lives in all of us and knows life is meant to be lived and experienced... marketing genius.

In this life, you are never stuck. One of my students, who drives trucks, used to be homeless, so he has been on the lowest rung of the social ladder and could have easily remained there. He has since discovered with a CDL (aka drive, motivation, and action) you will never be jobless. He is also a purple belt in jiu-jitsu and part of a community of over 130 educated and loving people. This is a real time reminder that we are never relegated to our current situation, as our current situation is the culmination of past choices and motivations. But right now is called the present for a reason, as we have been gifted with another day to change our situation. This logic is no different for a drug addict, alcoholic or even an erstwhile criminal. I have known firsthand of felons who made a major mistake, paid their debt to society, and then reorganized their life and became incredibly successful people. Their past choices and actions are what lead them to today, but today will always be the day that everything can change. Every action could lead to laudable results if said actions encompass a motivation to be better and feel better.

If there is something you want to achieve or accomplish, go out and do it. Do not give power or pay credence to what others say or believe about your potential. A friend of mine, who is a good medic, but lacks actual years of experience was pondering the idea of being an FTO (field training officer), but afraid of what people would think. I told her this thinking was superficial and she should not give energy to such thoughts. I told her people who do not support you or who spread vitriol about you are like flies, they are an annoyance at best, so just ignore them and focus on yourself. If I gave credence to what people thought, I would never have had the courage to publish this book or allow it to leave my laptop. You must surrender the results and go for it, whatever it is that you want to accomplish. The universe rewards risk takers and will allow everyone else to remain exactly where they are, stuck!

Also, I have only been in the fire service for eight and half years (with a year off), and I am considering applying for the next Lieutenant position. There are many others (I heard there are over forty others eligible), some with more time in and more certifications than me, but that does not intimidate me. If I make the choice to join the process, I will do what is necessary to win the position and believe in my ability to focus and win. If for some reason the powers that be told me no, I would say okay next.

Never dwell on the losses but learn from them. They are a source for growth and improvement. As for me, I will also help others and utilize the power of focus, effort and creation as opposed to competition to achieve greatness. With taking chances in life, I recommend drawing a line in the sand...accept your worst-case scenario. Worst case, I end up where I am right now, which isn't too bad. "Make them tell you no." is my philosophy.

If I focus my beliefs, and energy and match the intensity of my thoughts with the action of my body, achieving said goal will be a piece of cake. The author *Florence Scovel Shinn,* wrote a book about this called the *Game of Life and How to Play it,* and provides this quote *"You can control any situation if you first control yourself"*. For more insight into the secrets of life, I suggest you read this and other books like it, and please use my work as supplementation to your studies as a human being.

I sincerely thank those before me that had the courage to share their knowledge and experiences and thank God for allowing me the ability to create and share this work. As for anyone reading these lines, thank you from the heart for hearing me out and sharing your time with me. In the beginning of this book, I shared the following quote by Andrew Carnegie, *"Men with ideas write books that lift their fellows out of the depths of despair and give them a new start in life."* This certainly rings true for me, and my hope is that all the amazing works I have referenced in my book will do the same for you. Again, it has been my honor to write this book. Life is good, and I am thankful every day. Thank you for your time and be well. –Rob "Faith over Fear" 2021

# SOURCES

**CHAPTER ONE:**

Wattles, Wallace (2019) The Science of Getting Rich [E-Book] Connecticut, Gildan Media LLC

Dawson, Ted (2017) Sociopaths and Psychopaths [E-Book] Connecticut, We Can't Be Beat LLC.

Marrs, Jim (2010) The Trillion Dollar Conspiracy [E-Book] New York, HarperCollins e-books

**CHAPTER TWO:**

Dispenza, Joe (2017) Becoming Supernatural [E-Book] California, Hay House Inc.

The Secret, Directed by Drew Heriot, Screenplay by Rhonda Byrne, Prime Time Productions 2006

Sylvia, Claire & Novak, William (1998) A Change of Heart, New York, Warner Books Inc.

Hill, Napoleon (2018) How to Own Your Own Mind, [E-Book] India, Prabhat Books

Hill, Napoleon (2012) Outwitting the Devil, [E-Book] New York, Sterling Publishing

Grout, Pam (2013) E- Squared [E-Book] California, Hay House Inc.

Hill, Napoleon (2015) Think and Grow Rich, [E-Book] Connecticut, Gildan Media LLC

Hicks, Esther and Jerry (2006) Law of Attraction (The Basics of the Teachings of Abraham) California, Hay House Inc.

## CHAPTER THREE:

Griffin, Forrest & Erich Krauss (2009) Got Fight? New York, HarperCollins Publishers

Bernays, Edward (1928/1955/2005) Propaganda [E-Book] New York, Ig Publishing

Hill, Napoleon (2012) Outwitting the Devil [E-Book] New York, Sterling Publishing

Bradden, Greg (2007) The Divine Matrix [E-Book] California, Hay House Inc.

Proctor, Bob with Gallagher, Sandra (2015) The Art of Living [E-Book] New York, Penguin Random House LLC

Allen, James (1908) As a Man Thinketh Chicago, Sheldon University Press

## CHAPTER FIVE:

Hill, Napoleon (2018) How to Own Your Own Mind [E-Book] India, Prabhat Books

Kwik, Jim (2020) Limitless [E-Book] California, Hay House Inc.

## CHAPTER SEVEN:

I am not Your Guru, Directed by Joe Berlinger, Screenplay by Joe Berlinger by Netflix 2016

Rainn/ 2020, *Rainn Campus Sexual Violence Statistics,* Rainn.org (day viewed April 14 2021) {Rainn.org/statistics/campus-sexual-violence}

## CHAPTER NINE:

Proctor, Bob 2009, It's Not About the Money [E-Book] Toronto, Ontario BurmanBooks Inc.

## CHAPTER TEN:

Timeless Book (Uploaded April 30,2021) *The Secret of the 33 Degree Freemason https://www.youtube.com/watch?v=PsA-cBOV8ek&t=3294s*

Orwell, George (1949), Nineteen Eighty Four, New York, Penguin Publishing Group

Kwik, Jim (2020) Limitless [E-Book] California, Hay House Inc.

Ferry, Matthew (2018) Quiet Mind Epic Life [E-Book] Newport Beach, California, Spiritual Hooligan Publishing

## CHAPTER ELEVEN:

Hill, Napoleon, (2012) Outwitting the Devil [E-Book] New York, Sterling Publishing

Singh, Kanwer (Humble the Poet) (2019) Things No One Else Can Teach Us, California/New York, HarperOne

## CHAPTER TWELVE:

Asprey, Dave (2018) Game Changers [E-Book] New York, HarperCollins Publishing

WHO/ April 2020, *Obesity and Overweight, WHO (day viewed Mar 30, 2021) Who.int/news-room/fact-sheets/detail/obesity-and-overweight*

Ferriss, Tim (2016) Tools of Titans [E-Book] Boston/New York, Houghton Mifflin Harcourt


## CHAPTER THIRTEEN:

Tedx Talks (Jan 9, 2016) *Unwavering Focus/ Dandapani/ Tedx Reno https:// www.youtube.com/watch?v=4O2JK_94g3Y*

Andrew Perrin Sep 26, 2019, *Who Doesn't Read Books in America,* Pew Research Center, (viewed in February 2021) *pewresearch.org/ fact-tank/2019/09/26/who-doesn't-read-books-in-america/*

Anonymous, 2014, Silent Weapons for Quiet wars [E-Book/Kindle]

Kwik, Jim 2020, Limitless [E-Book] California, Hay House Inc.

Orwell, George (1949) Nineteen Eighty Four New York, Penguin Publishing Group

Haisch, Bernard (2009) The God Theory [E-Book] California, Red Wheel/ Weiser, LLC

Globetrotters in Action (uploaded Nov 2, 2020) *"Create Something" Workshop with Christian Graugart* Youtube.com/ watch?v=gqtTRF5Fu98&t=1682s

Mandino, O.G. (1972/78) The Greatest Secret in The World New York, Bantam Books

Marrs, Jim (2010) Trillion Dollar Conspiracy [E-book] New York, HarperCollins e-books

## CHAPTER FOURTEEN:

Lakoff, George (2004) Don't Think Like an Elephant [E-Book] Hartford, VT Chelsea Green Publishing

EFSGV (January 2021) *Virginia Gun Deaths: 2019* (Viewed Feb 2021) efsgv.org/state/virginia

## CHAPTER FIFTEEN:

Wehrwein, Peter (March 2020) *Astounding Increase in Antidepressant Use by Americans,* Harvard Health Publishing (viewed March 2021) https://www.health.harvard.edu/blog/astounding-increase-in-antidepressant-use-by-americans-201110203624

Thiel, Peter (2014) Zero to One [E-Book] New York, Crown Publishing Group

Carufel, Richard (Mar 18 2019) *The Most Stressful Jobs of 2019, Agility PR Solutions, (Viewed Feb 2021) https://www.agilitypr.com/pr-news/public-relations/the-most-stressful-jobs-of-2019-pr-executive-ranked-among-top-10/*

Dispenza, Joe (2017) Becoming Supernatural [E-Book] California, Hay House Inc.

Forster, E.M. (1909) The Machine Stops (short story) The Oxford and Cambridge Review

Hill, Napoleon, (2012) Outwitting the Devil [E-Book] New York, Sterling Publishing

Isaacson, Walter (2004) Benjamin franklin, An American Life [E-Book] New York, Simon and Schuster

## CHAPTER NINETEEN:

Factmonster Staff,(Feb 21, 2017) *Facts About U.S. Money,* Fact Monster, (Viewed Feb 2021) https://www.factmonster.com/math/money/facts-about-us-money#:~:text=How%20much%20money%20is%20printed,value%20of%20approximately%20%24541%20million.

Wattles, Wallace (2019) The Science of Getting Rich [E-Book] Connecticut, Gildan Media LLC

Amadeo, Kimberly (April 7, 2021) Website: The blance.com Article: Who owns the national debt (Viewed March 2021) https://www.thebalance.com/who-owns-the-u-s-national-debt-3306124

Hill, Napoleon, (2012) Outwitting the Devil [E-Book] New York, Sterling Publishing

Hill, Napoleon (2015) Think and Grow Rich, [E-Book] Connecticut, Gildan Media LLC

Ingraham, Christopher (Dec 6, 2017) *The Richest one Percent Now Owns More of the Countries Wealth Than Any Time in the Past 50 Years (viewed Jan 2021)* The Washington Post https://www.washingtonpost.com/news/wonk/wp/2017/12/06/the-richest-1-percent-now-owns-more-of-the-countrys-wealth-than-at-any-time-in-the-past-50-years/

Andrews, Andy (2008) The Seven Decisions, [E-Book] Tennessee, W Publishing Group

## CHAPTER TWENTY:

Heart Math Institute 2012-2021 https://www.heartmath.org/resources/videos/mysteries-of-the-heart/

I am not Your Guru, Directed by Joe Berlinger, Screenplay by Joe Berlinger by Netflix 2016

Dispenza, Joe (2017) Becoming Supernatural [E-Book] California, Hay House Inc.

## CHAPTER TWENTY-ONE:

Scovel Shinn, Florence (2015) The Game of Life and How to Play it Charlottesville VA, Hampton Roads Publishing Company, Inc

—